PROLOGUE:

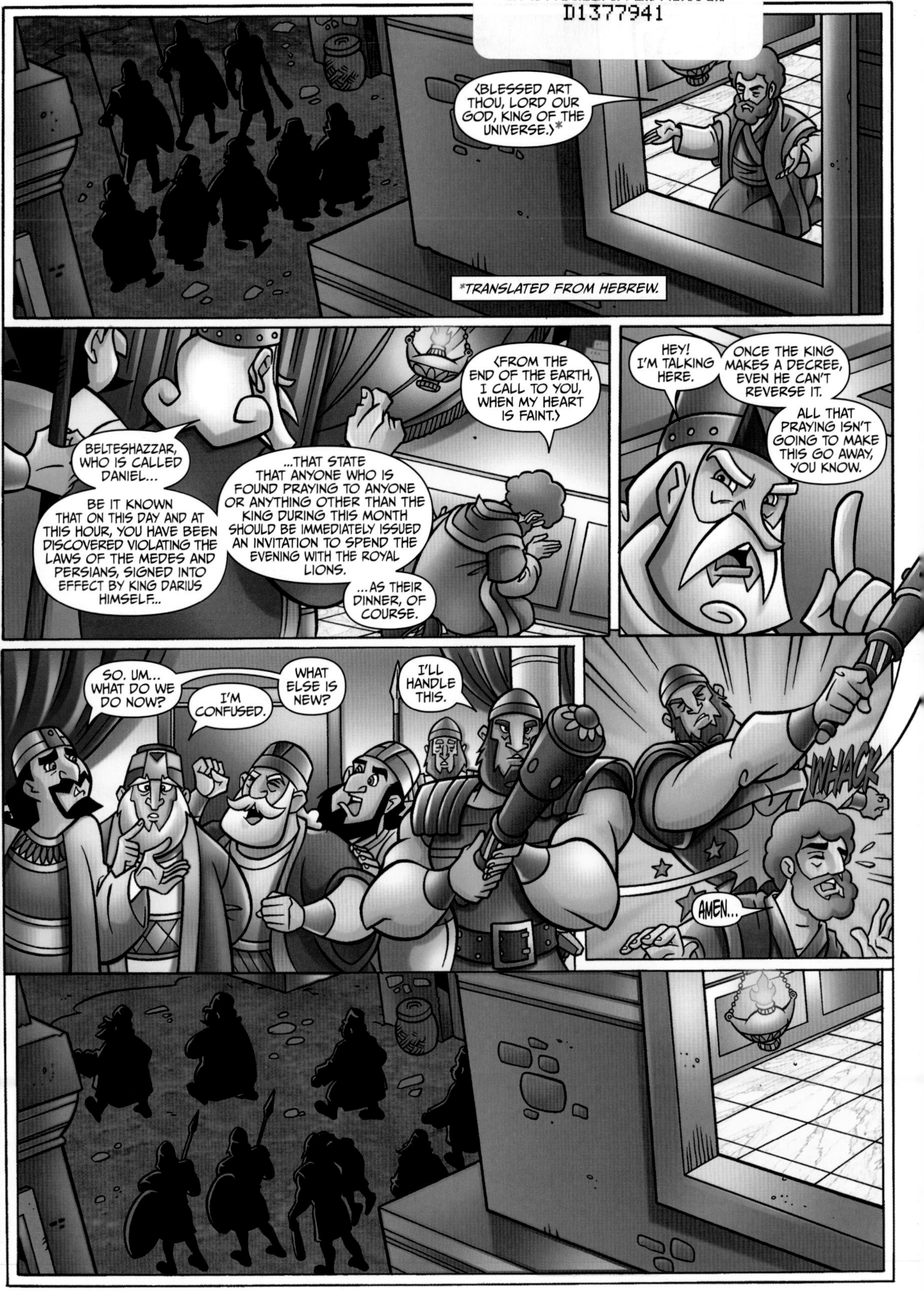

<BLESSED ART THOU, LORD OUR GOD, KING OF THE UNIVERSE.>*
*TRANSLATED FROM HEBREW.
<FROM THE END OF THE EARTH, I CALL TO YOU, WHEN MY HEART IS FAINT.>
BELTESHAZZAR, WHO IS CALLED DANIEL...
BE IT KNOWN THAT ON THIS DAY AND AT THIS HOUR, YOU HAVE BEEN DISCOVERED VIOLATING THE LAWS OF THE MEDES AND PERSIANS, SIGNED INTO EFFECT BY KING DARIUS HIMSELF...
...THAT STATE THAT ANYONE WHO IS FOUND PRAYING TO ANYONE OR ANYTHING OTHER THAN THE KING DURING THIS MONTH SHOULD BE IMMEDIATELY ISSUED AN INVITATION TO SPEND THE EVENING WITH THE ROYAL LIONS.
...AS THEIR DINNER, OF COURSE.
HEY! I'M TALKING HERE.
ONCE THE KING MAKES A DECREE, EVEN HE CAN'T REVERSE IT.
ALL THAT PRAYING ISN'T GOING TO MAKE THIS GO AWAY, YOU KNOW.
SO. UM... WHAT DO WE DO NOW?
I'M CONFUSED.
WHAT ELSE IS NEW?
I'LL HANDLE THIS.
WHACK
AMEN...

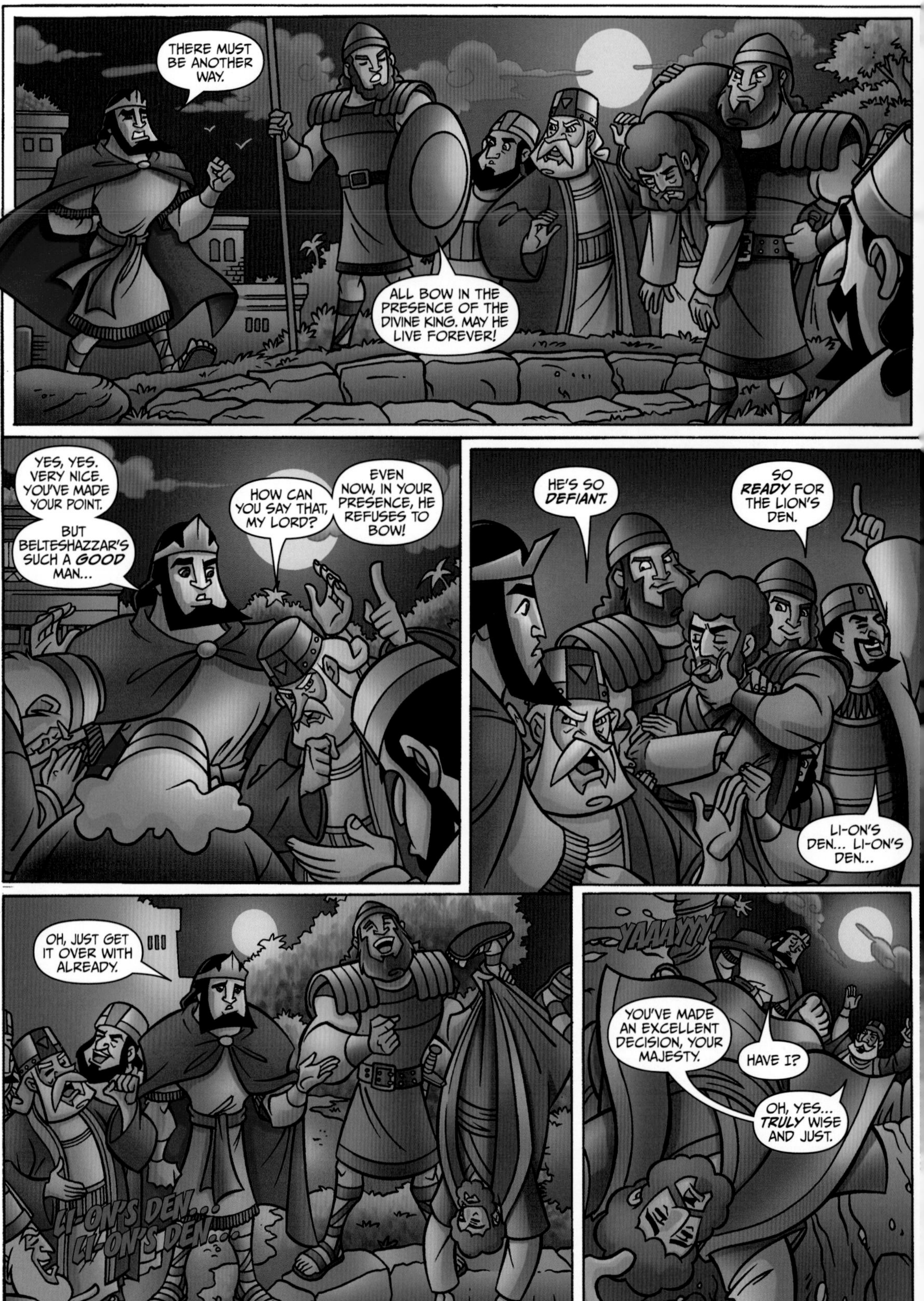
THERE MUST BE ANOTHER WAY.
ALL BOW IN THE PRESENCE OF THE DIVINE KING. MAY HE LIVE FOREVER!
YES, YES. VERY NICE. YOU'VE MADE YOUR POINT.
BUT BELTESHAZZAR'S SUCH A GOOD MAN...
HOW CAN YOU SAY THAT, MY LORD?
EVEN NOW, IN YOUR PRESENCE, HE REFUSES TO BOW!
HE'S SO DEFIANT.
SO READY FOR THE LION'S DEN.
LI-ON'S DEN... LI-ON'S DEN...
OH, JUST GET IT OVER WITH ALREADY.
LI-ON'S DEN...
LI-ON'S DEN...
YAAAYYY!
YOU'VE MADE AN EXCELLENT DECISION, YOUR MAJESTY.
HAVE I?
OH, YES... TRULY WISE AND JUST.

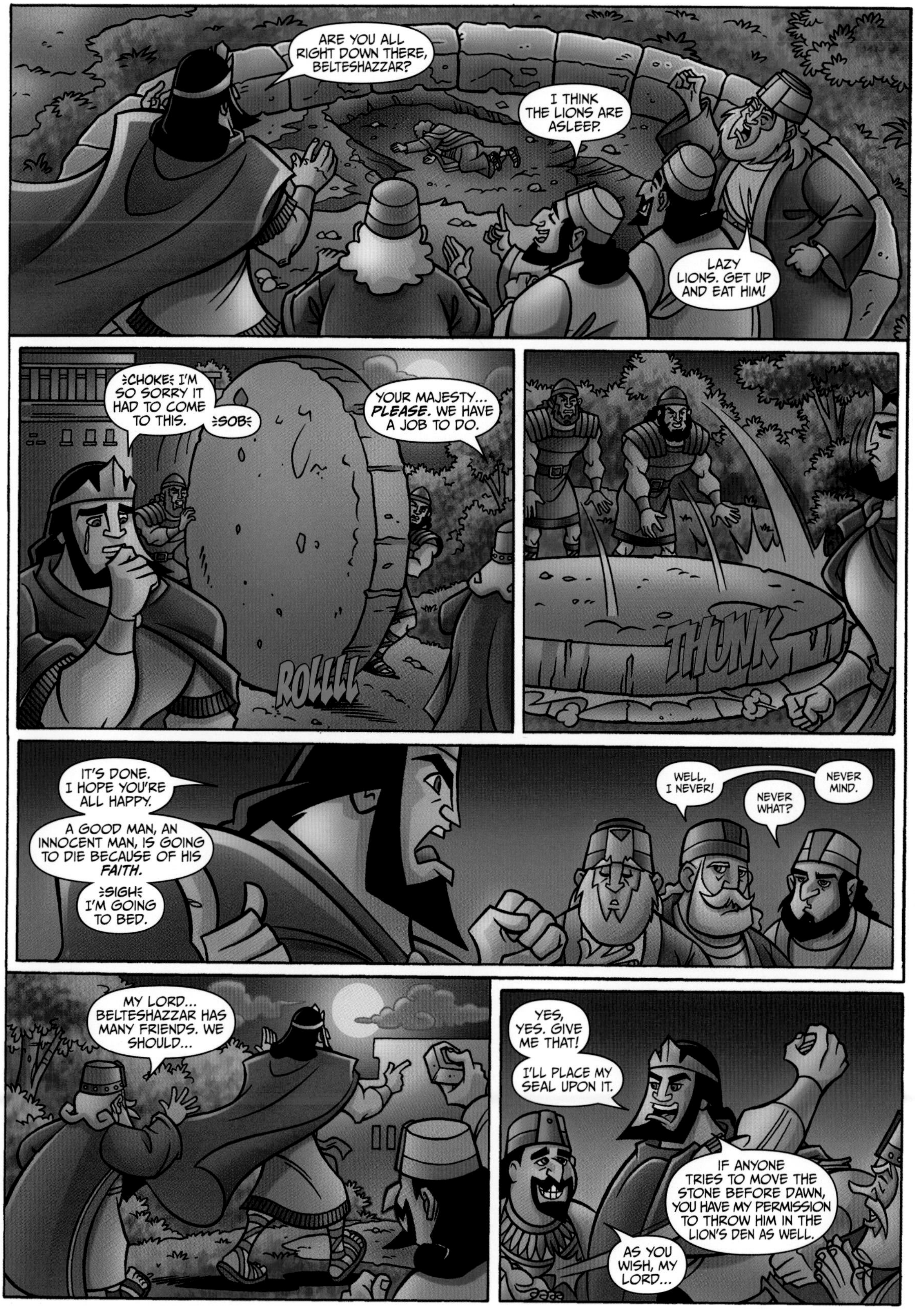
ARE YOU ALL RIGHT DOWN THERE, BELTESHAZZAR?
I THINK THE LIONS ARE ASLEEP.
LAZY LIONS. GET UP AND EAT HIM!
CHOKE I'M SO SORRY IT HAD TO COME TO THIS.
SOB
YOUR MAJESTY... **PLEASE.** WE HAVE A JOB TO DO.
ROLLLL
THUNK
IT'S DONE. I HOPE YOU'RE ALL HAPPY.
A GOOD MAN, AN INNOCENT MAN, IS GOING TO DIE BECAUSE OF HIS ***FAITH.***
SIGH I'M GOING TO BED.
WELL, I NEVER!
NEVER WHAT?
NEVER MIND.
MY LORD... BELTESHAZZAR HAS MANY FRIENDS. WE SHOULD...
YES, YES. GIVE ME THAT!
I'LL PLACE MY SEAL UPON IT.
IF ANYONE TRIES TO MOVE THE STONE BEFORE DAWN, YOU HAVE MY PERMISSION TO THROW HIM IN THE LION'S DEN AS WELL.
AS YOU WISH, MY LORD...

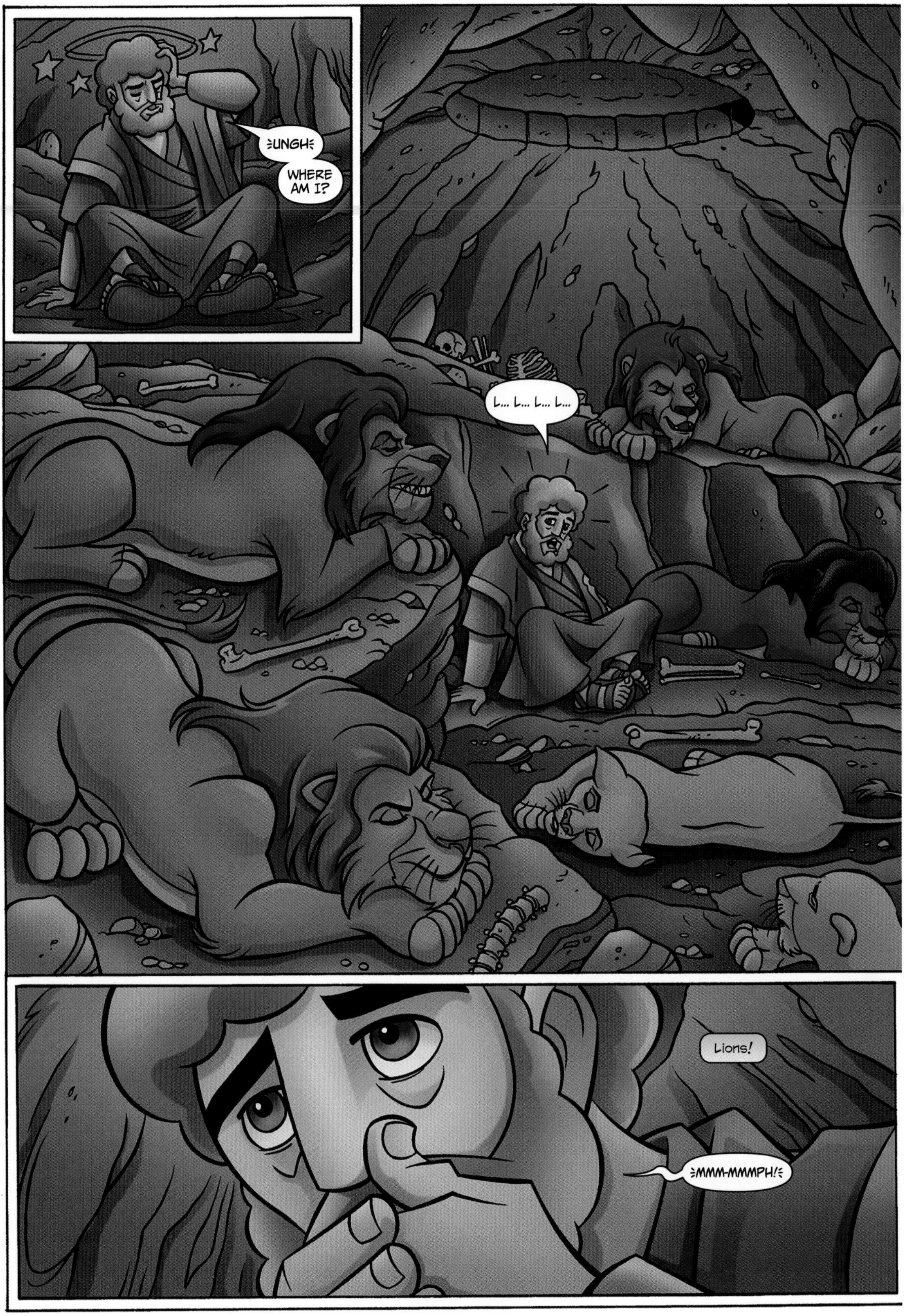
UNGH
WHERE AM I?
L... L... L... L...
Lions!
MMM-MMMPH!

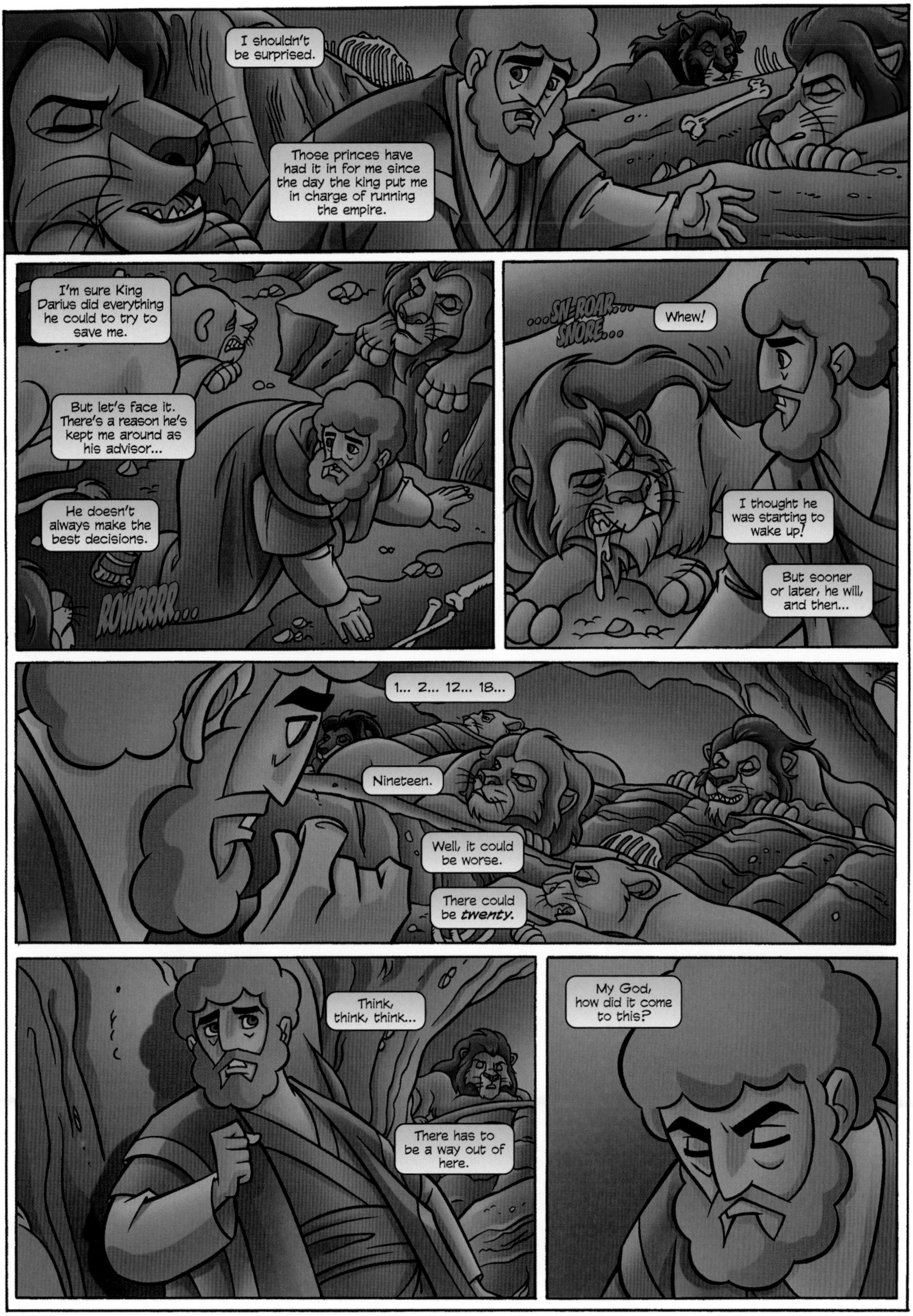
I shouldn't be surprised.
Those princes have had it in for me since the day the king put me in charge of running the empire.
I'm sure King Darius did everything he could to try to save me.
But let's face it. There's a reason he's kept me around as his advisor...
He doesn't always make the best decisions.
ROWRRRR...
...SN-ROAR... SNORE...
Whew!
I thought he was starting to wake up!
But sooner or later, he will, and then...
1... 2... 12... 18...
Nineteen.
Well, it could be worse.
There could be *twenty.*
Think, think, think...
There has to be a way out of here.
My God, how did it come to this?

CHAPTER 1: THE FALL OF JERUSALEM

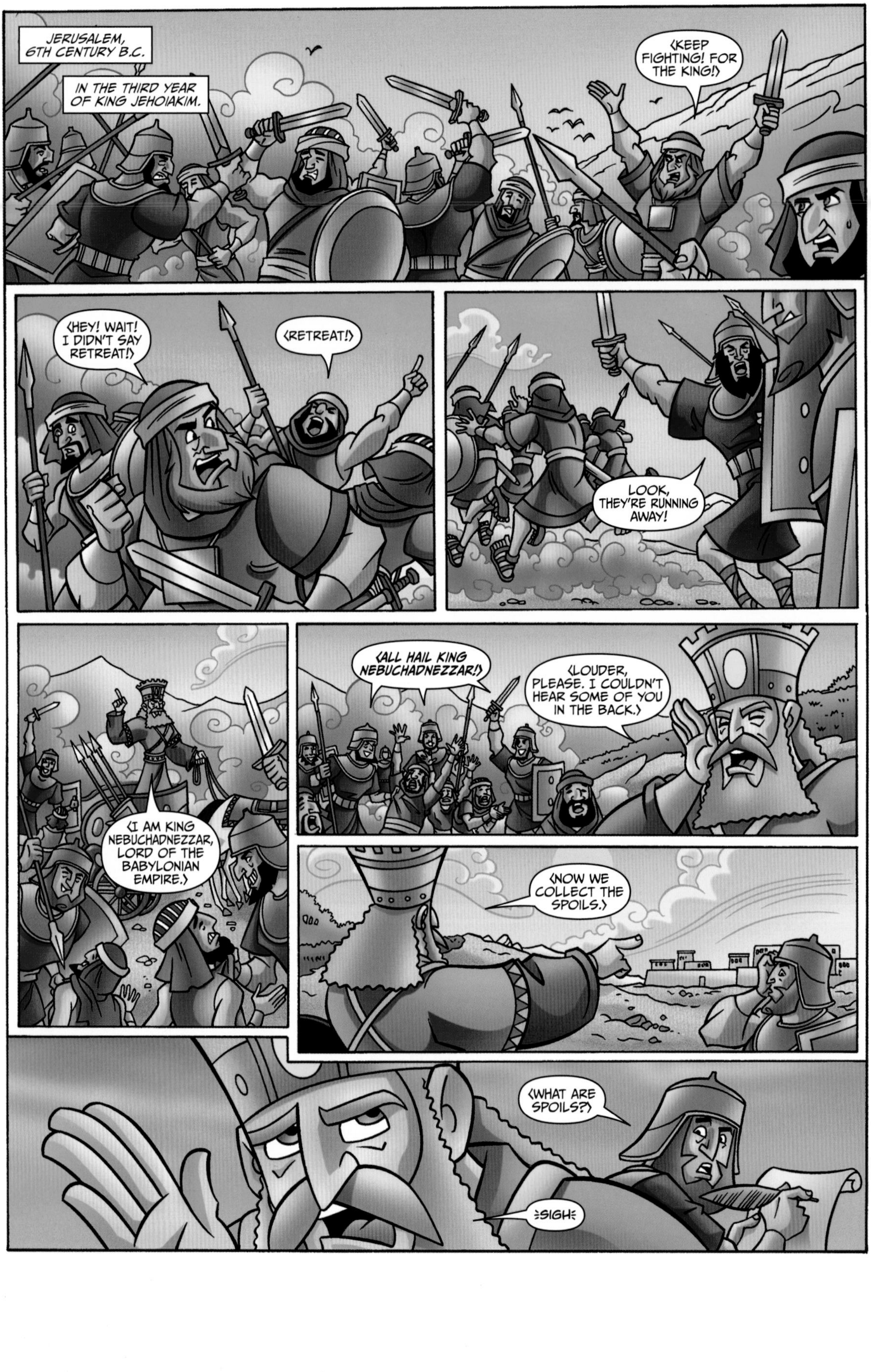

JERUSALEM, 6TH CENTURY B.C.
IN THE THIRD YEAR OF KING JEHOIAKIM.
‹KEEP FIGHTING! FOR THE KING!›
‹HEY! WAIT! I DIDN'T SAY RETREAT!›
‹RETREAT!›
LOOK, THEY'RE RUNNING AWAY!
‹I AM KING NEBUCHADNEZZAR, LORD OF THE BABYLONIAN EMPIRE.›
‹ALL HAIL KING NEBUCHADNEZZAR!›
‹LOUDER, PLEASE. I COULDN'T HEAR SOME OF YOU IN THE BACK.›
‹NOW WE COLLECT THE SPOILS.›
‹WHAT ARE SPOILS?›
⁝SIGH⁝

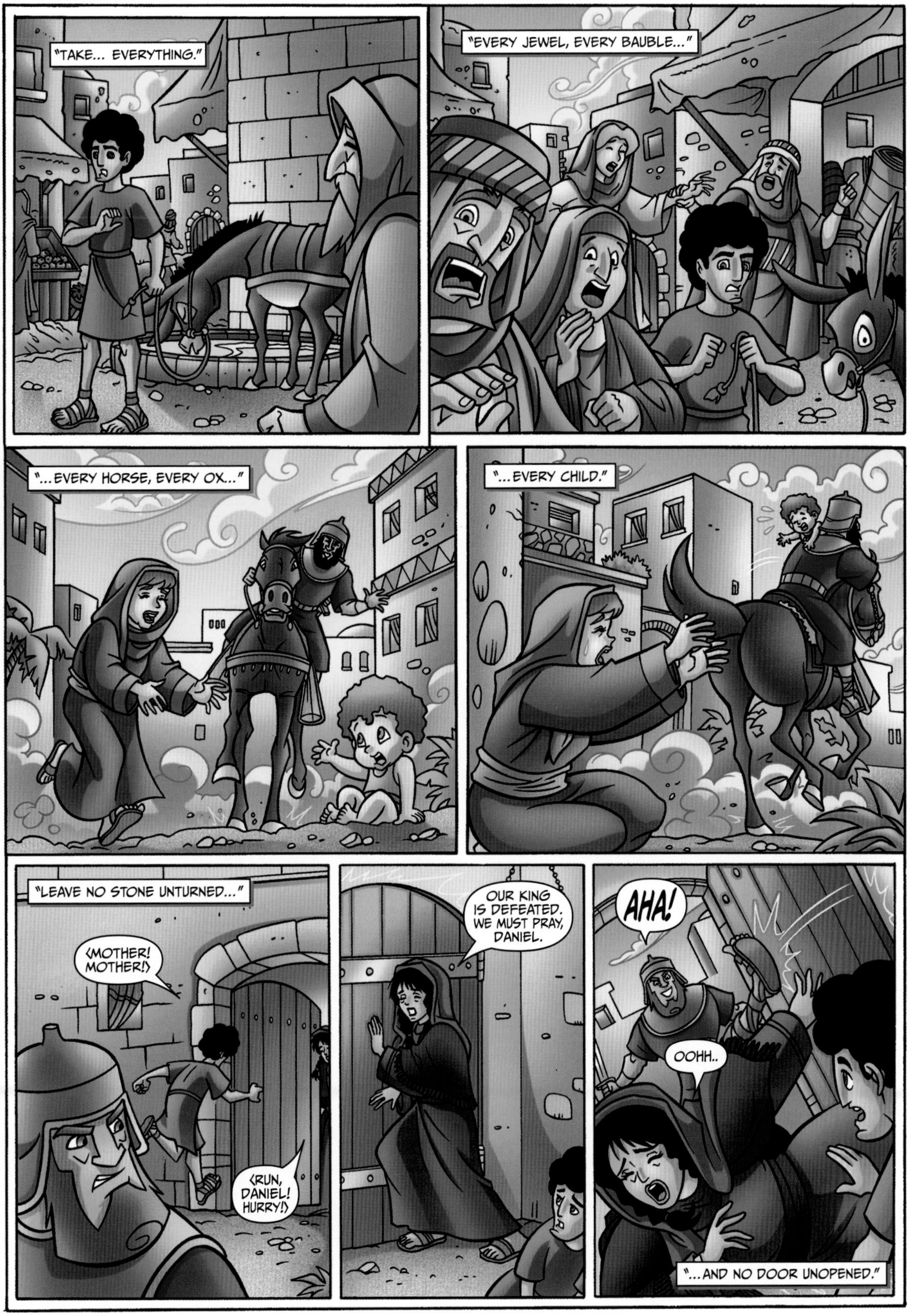
"TAKE... EVERYTHING."
"EVERY JEWEL, EVERY BAUBLE..."
"...EVERY HORSE, EVERY OX..."
"...EVERY CHILD."
"LEAVE NO STONE UNTURNED..."
‹MOTHER! MOTHER!›
‹RUN, DANIEL! HURRY!›
OUR KING IS DEFEATED. WE MUST PRAY, DANIEL.
AHA!
OOHH..
"...AND NO DOOR UNOPENED."

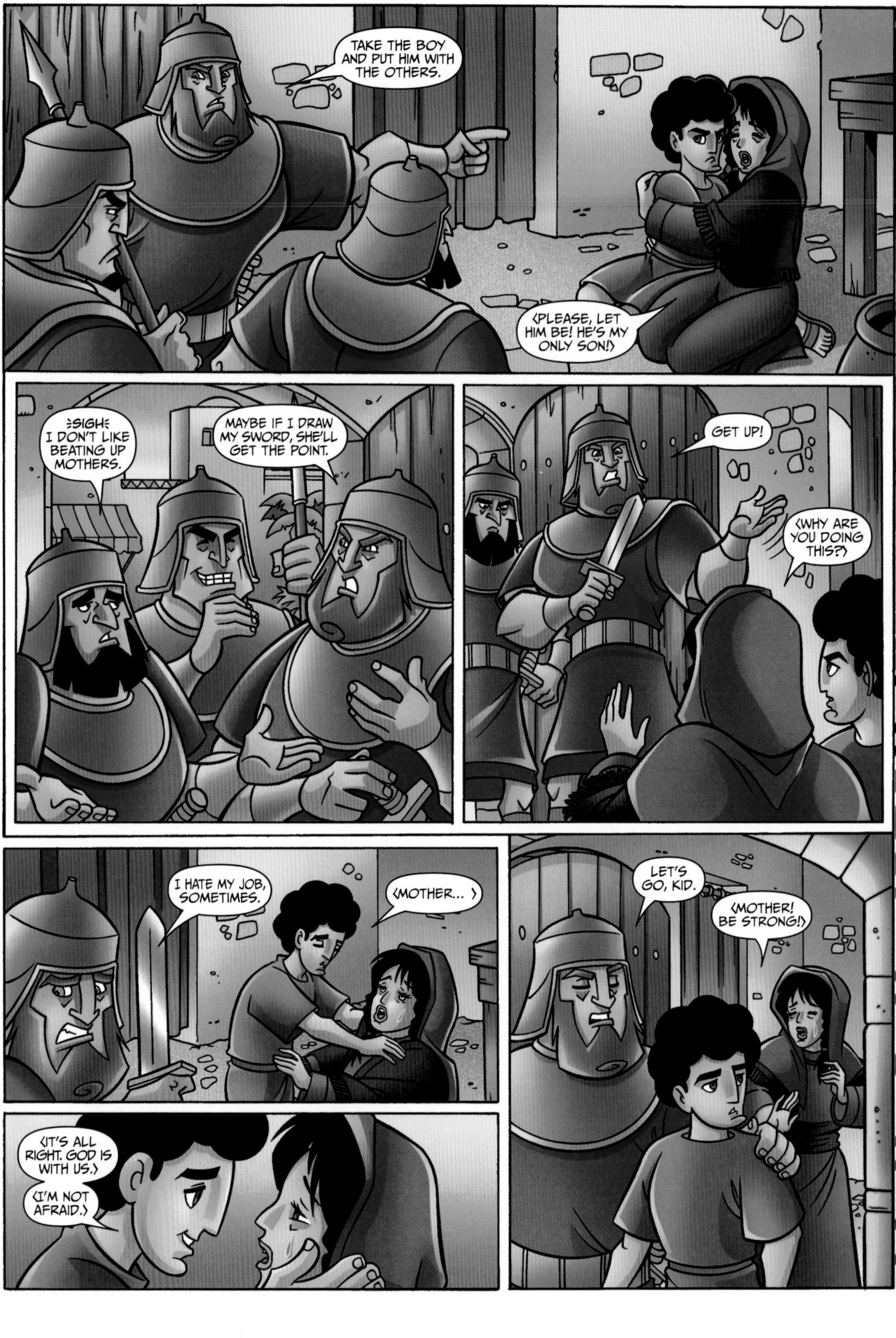
TAKE THE BOY AND PUT HIM WITH THE OTHERS.
‹PLEASE, LET HIM BE! HE'S MY ONLY SON!›
⩵SIGH⩵ I DON'T LIKE BEATING UP MOTHERS.
MAYBE IF I DRAW MY SWORD, SHE'LL GET THE POINT.
GET UP!
‹WHY ARE YOU DOING THIS?›
I HATE MY JOB, SOMETIMES.
‹MOTHER... ›
‹IT'S ALL RIGHT. GOD IS WITH US.›
‹I'M NOT AFRAID.›
LET'S GO, KID.
‹MOTHER! BE STRONG!›

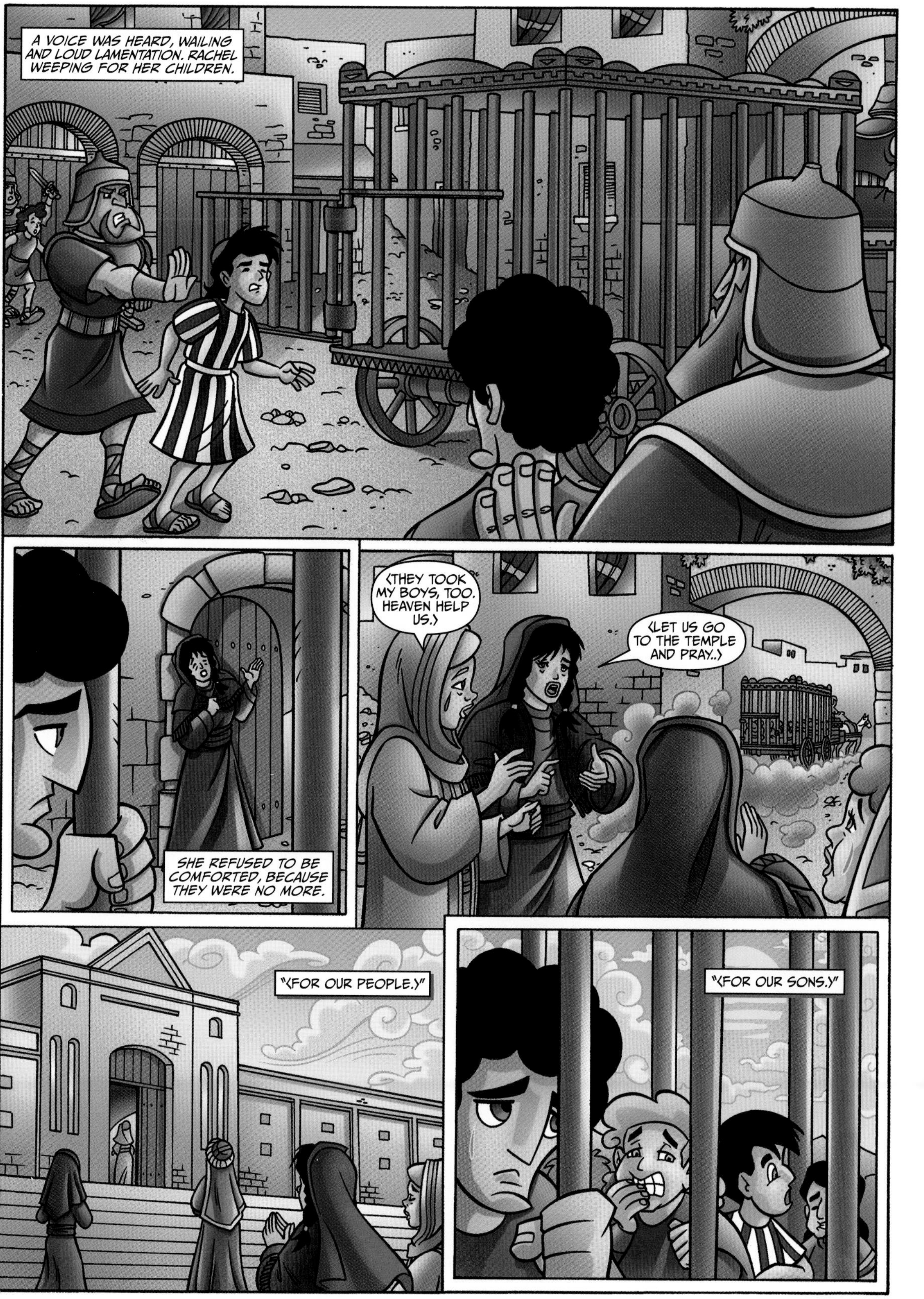
A VOICE WAS HEARD, WAILING AND LOUD LAMENTATION. RACHEL WEEPING FOR HER CHILDREN.
SHE REFUSED TO BE COMFORTED, BECAUSE THEY WERE NO MORE.
‹THEY TOOK MY BOYS, TOO. HEAVEN HELP US.›
‹LET US GO TO THE TEMPLE AND PRAY..›
"‹FOR OUR PEOPLE.›"
"‹FOR OUR SONS.›"

CHAPTER 2: SERVANTS OF BABYLON

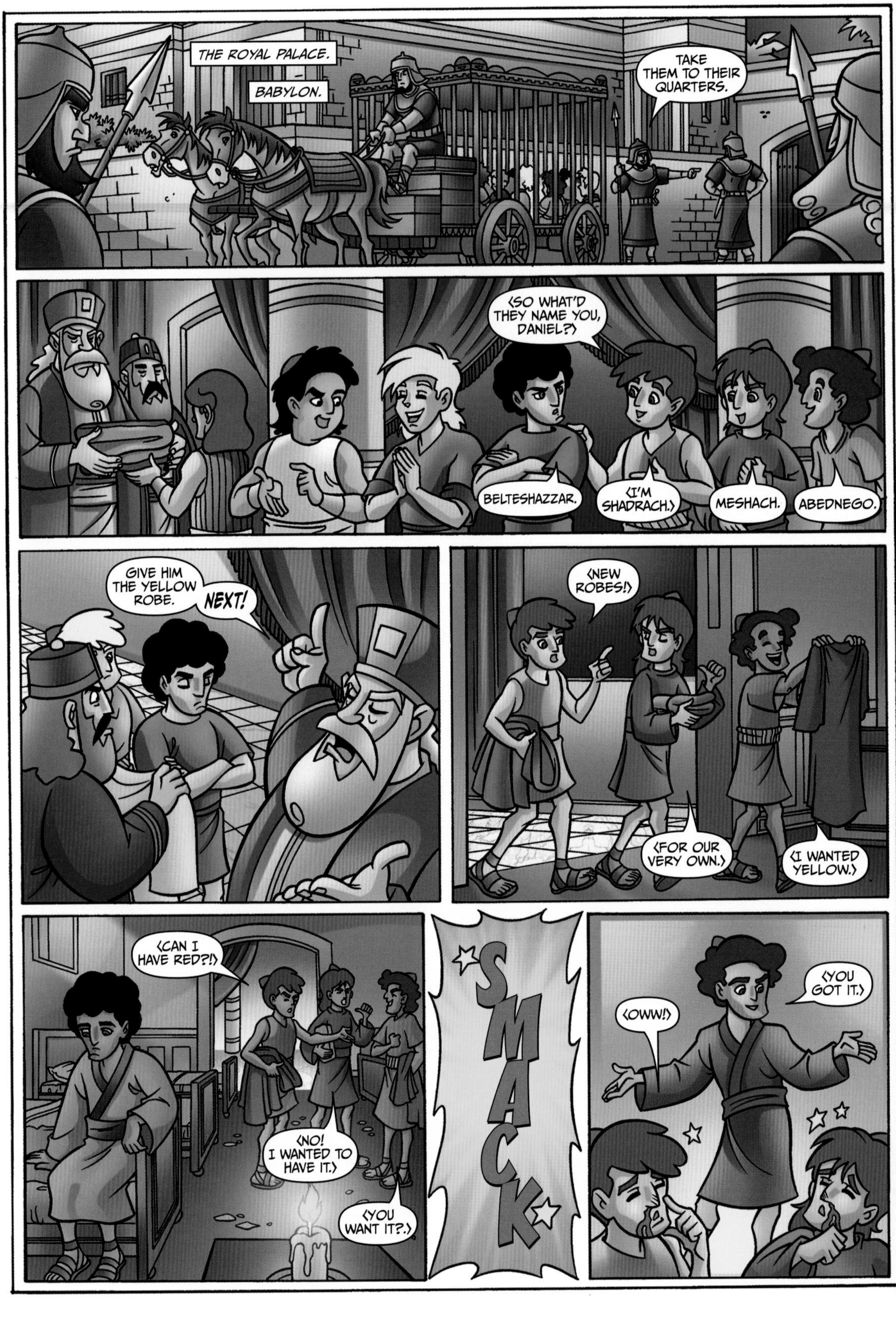
THE ROYAL PALACE.
BABYLON.
TAKE THEM TO THEIR QUARTERS.
‹SO WHAT'D THEY NAME YOU, DANIEL?›
BELTESHAZZAR.
‹I'M SHADRACH.›
MESHACH.
ABEDNEGO.
GIVE HIM THE YELLOW ROBE.
NEXT!
‹NEW ROBES!›
‹FOR OUR VERY OWN.›
‹I WANTED YELLOW.›
‹CAN I HAVE RED?!›
‹NO! I WANTED TO HAVE IT.›
‹YOU WANT IT?.›
SMACK
‹YOU GOT IT.›
‹OWW!›

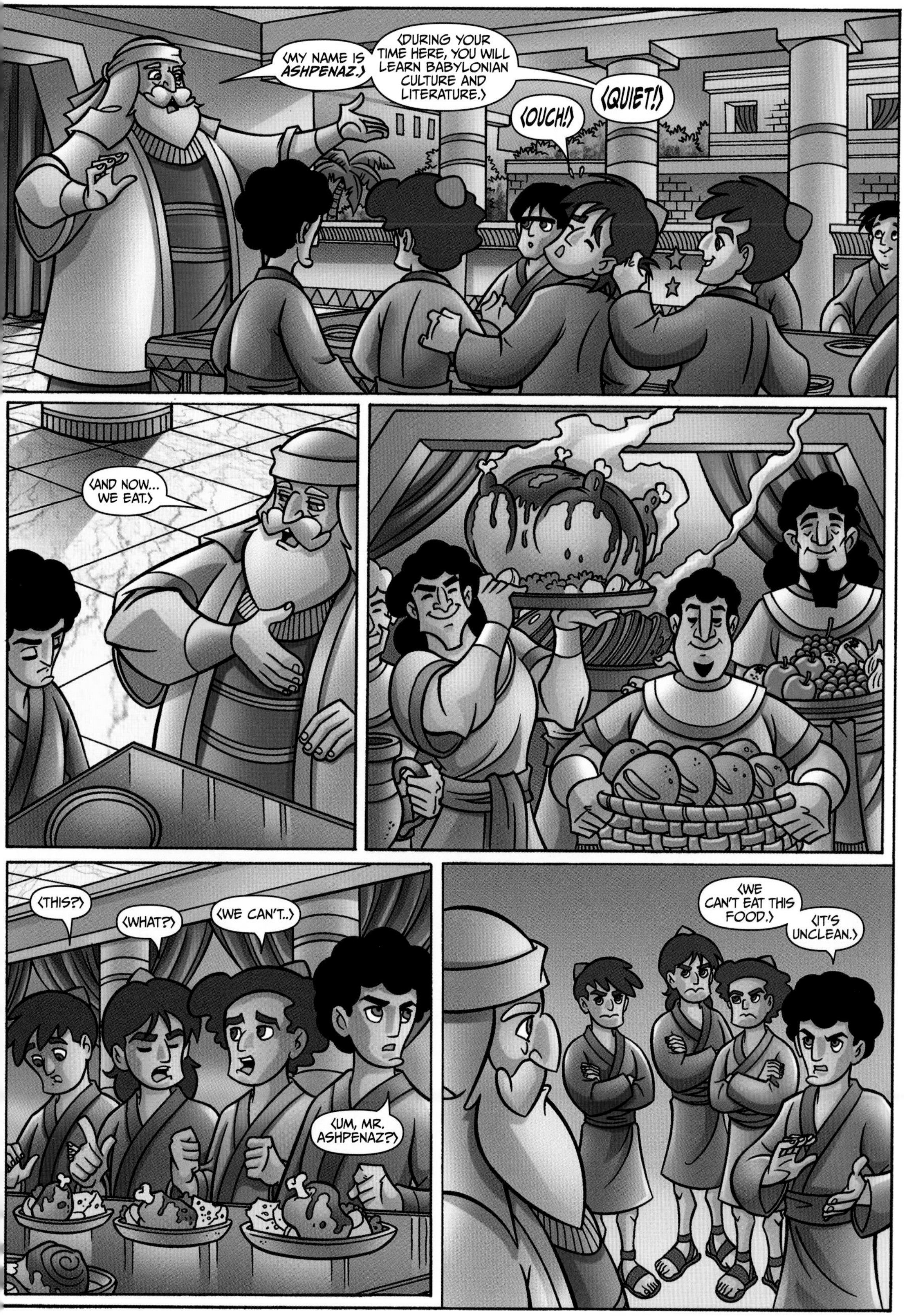
‹MY NAME IS *ASHPENAZ.*›
‹DURING YOUR TIME HERE, YOU WILL LEARN BABYLONIAN CULTURE AND LITERATURE.›
‹QUIET!›
‹OUCH!›
‹AND NOW... WE EAT.›
‹THIS?›
‹WHAT?›
‹WE CAN'T..›
‹UM, MR. ASHPENAZ?›
‹WE CAN'T EAT THIS FOOD.›
‹IT'S UNCLEAN.›

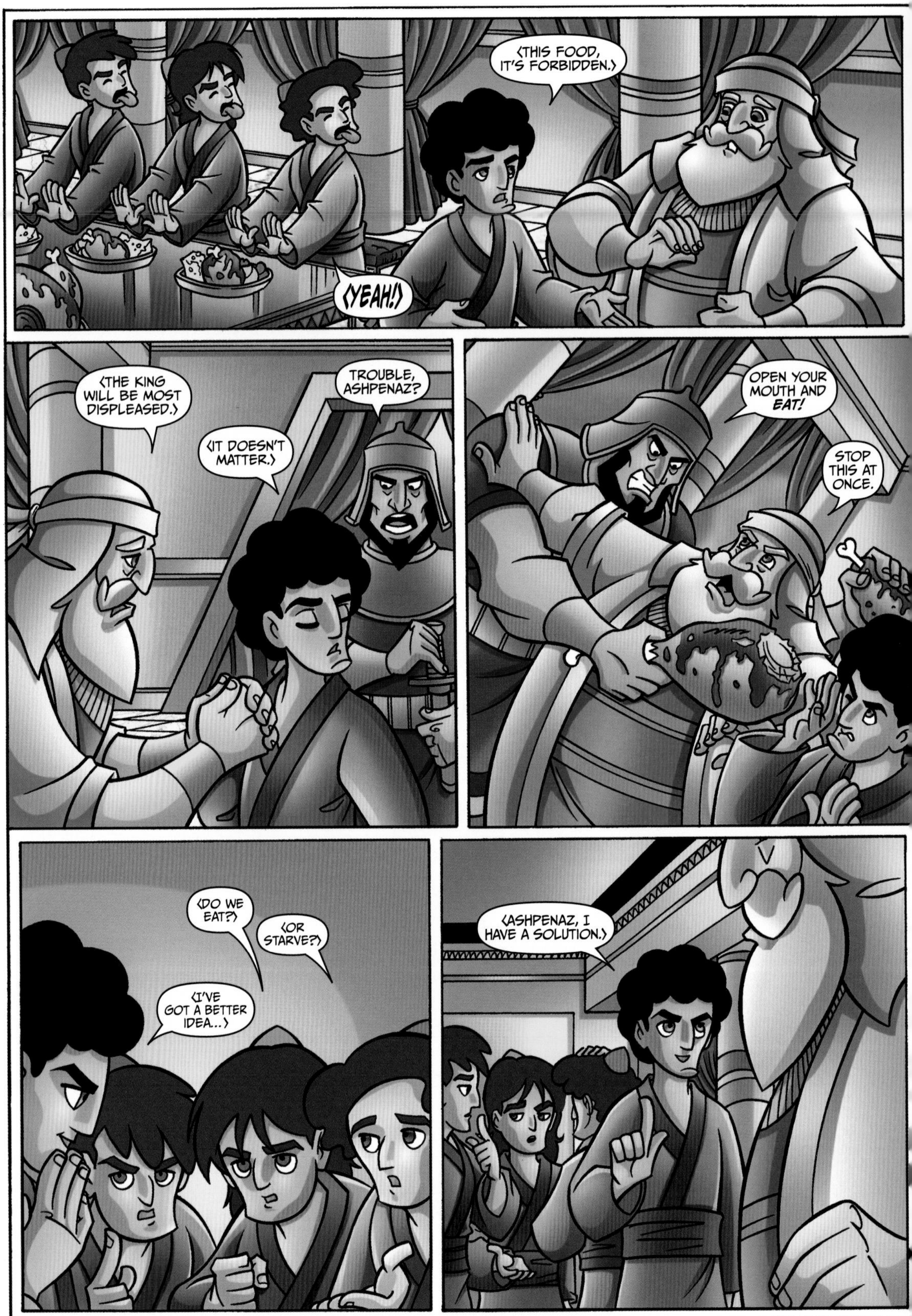

‹THIS FOOD, IT'S FORBIDDEN.›
‹YEAH!›
‹THE KING WILL BE MOST DISPLEASED.›
TROUBLE, ASHPENAZ?
‹IT DOESN'T MATTER.›
OPEN YOUR MOUTH AND *EAT!*
STOP THIS AT ONCE.
‹DO WE EAT?›
‹OR STARVE?›
‹I'VE GOT A BETTER IDEA...›
‹ASHPENAZ, I HAVE A SOLUTION.›

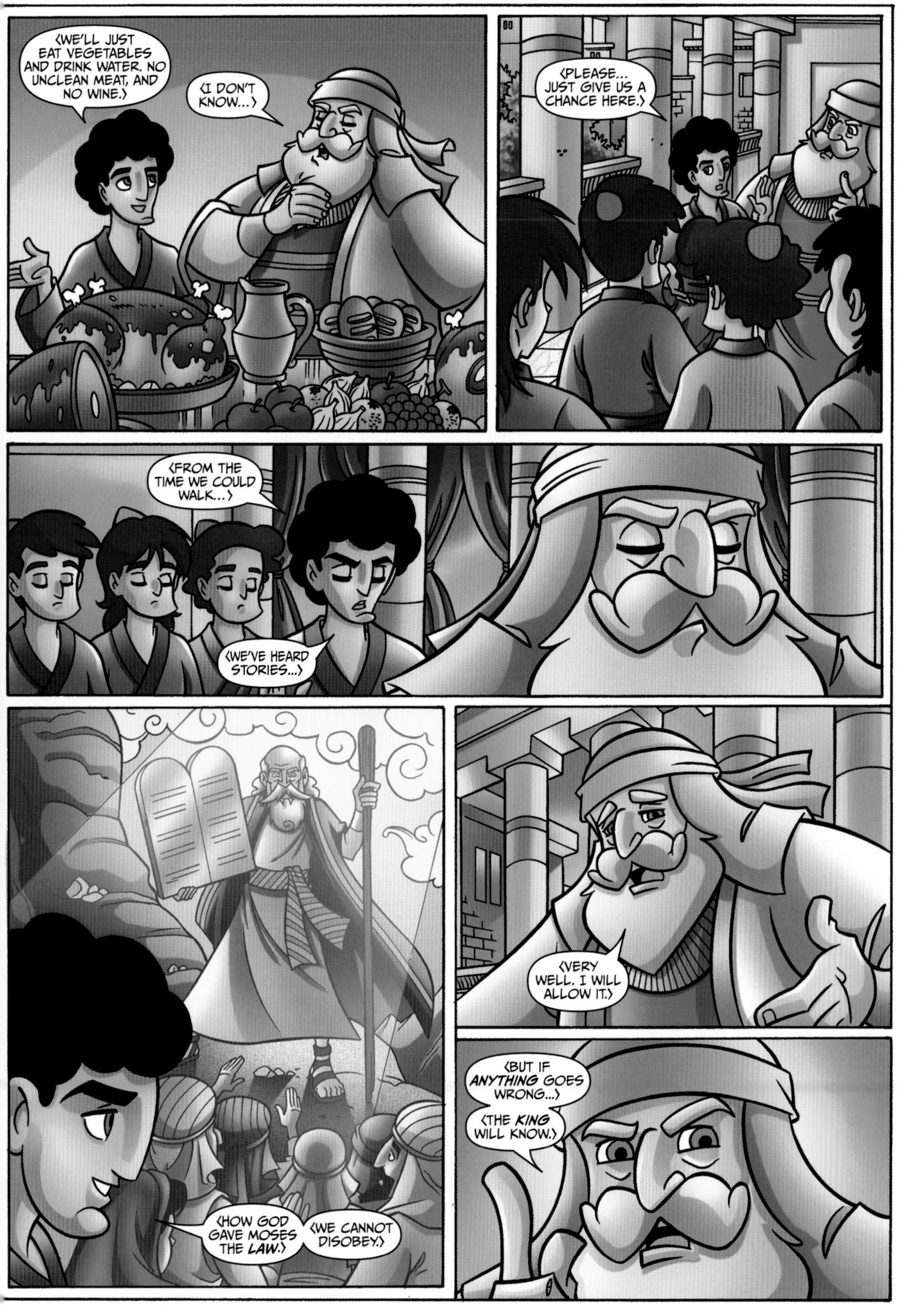
‹WE'LL JUST EAT VEGETABLES AND DRINK WATER. NO UNCLEAN MEAT, AND NO WINE.›
‹I DON'T KNOW...›
‹PLEASE... JUST GIVE US A CHANCE HERE.›
‹FROM THE TIME WE COULD WALK...›
‹WE'VE HEARD STORIES...›
‹HOW GOD GAVE MOSES THE *LAW*.›
‹WE CANNOT DISOBEY.›
‹VERY WELL. I WILL ALLOW IT.›
‹BUT IF *ANYTHING* GOES WRONG...›
‹THE *KING* WILL KNOW.›

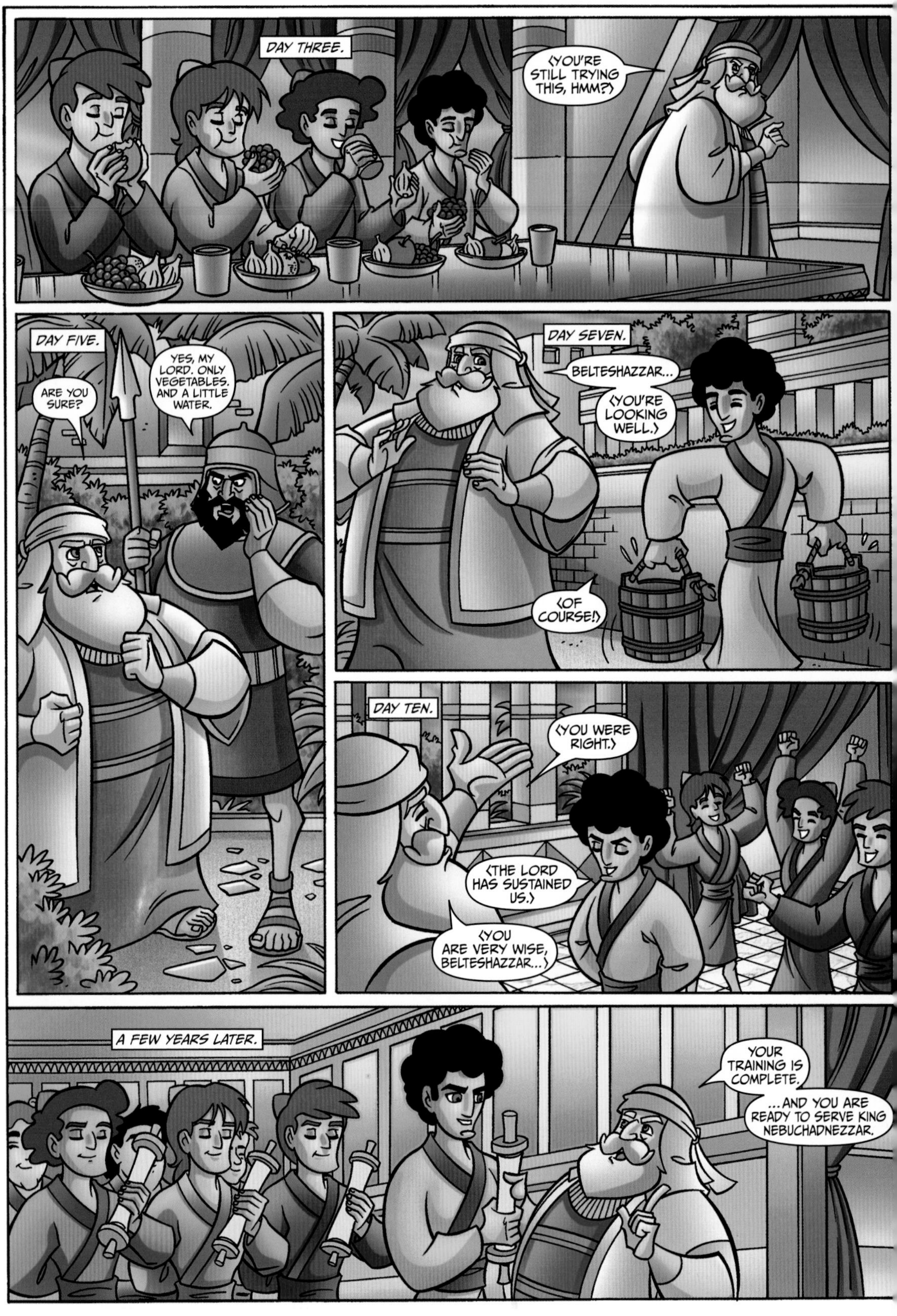
DAY THREE.
‹YOU'RE STILL TRYING THIS, HMM?›
DAY FIVE.
ARE YOU SURE?
YES, MY LORD. ONLY VEGETABLES. AND A LITTLE WATER.
DAY SEVEN.
BELTESHAZZAR...
‹YOU'RE LOOKING WELL.›
‹OF COURSE!›
DAY TEN.
‹YOU WERE RIGHT.›
‹THE LORD HAS SUSTAINED US.›
‹YOU ARE VERY WISE, BELTESHAZZAR...›
A FEW YEARS LATER.
YOUR TRAINING IS COMPLETE.
...AND YOU ARE READY TO SERVE KING NEBUCHADNEZZAR.

CHAPTER 3: THE DREAMER KING

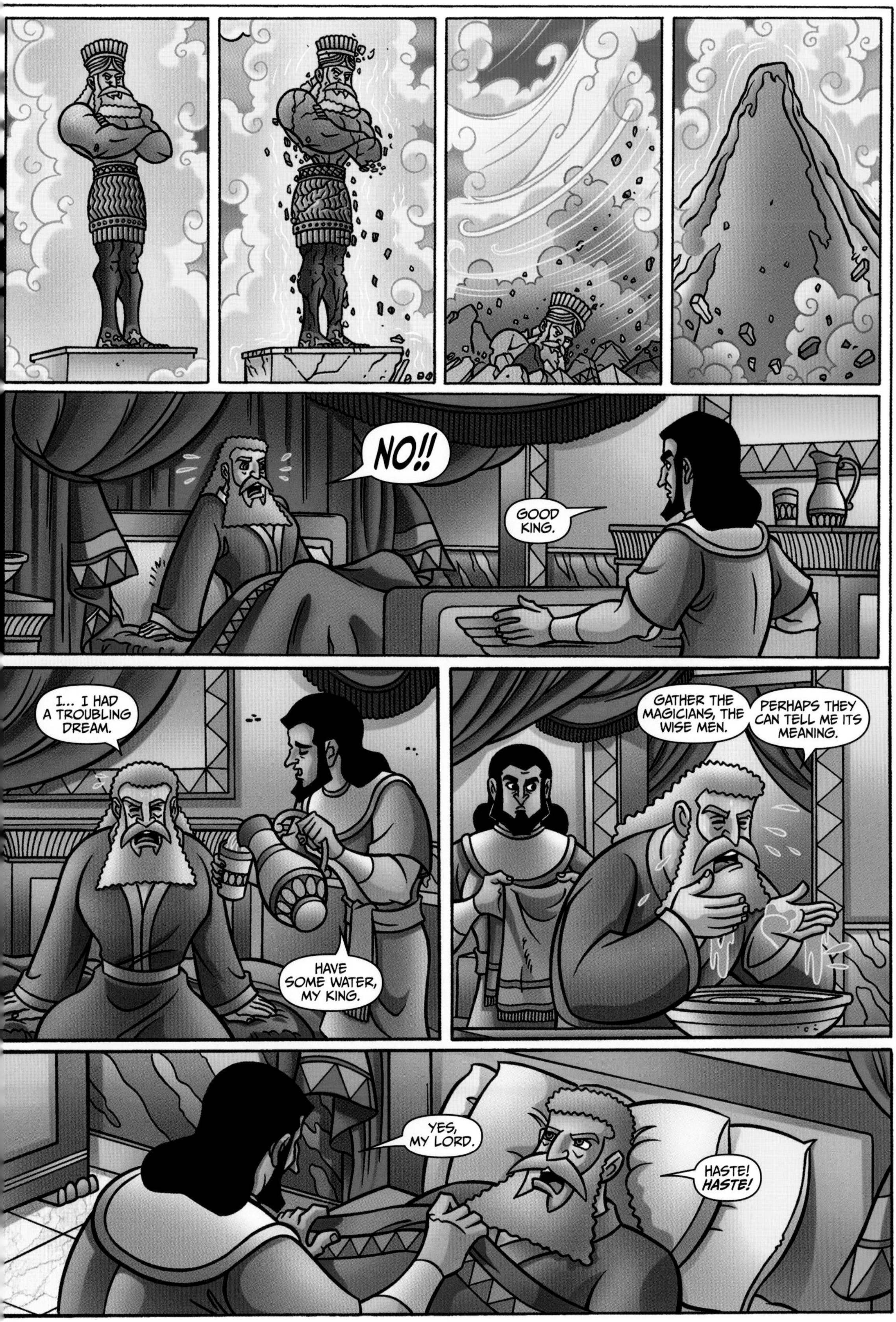
NO!!
GOOD KING.
I... I HAD A TROUBLING DREAM.
HAVE SOME WATER, MY KING.
GATHER THE MAGICIANS, THE WISE MEN.
PERHAPS THEY CAN TELL ME ITS MEANING.
YES, MY LORD.
HASTE! *HASTE!*

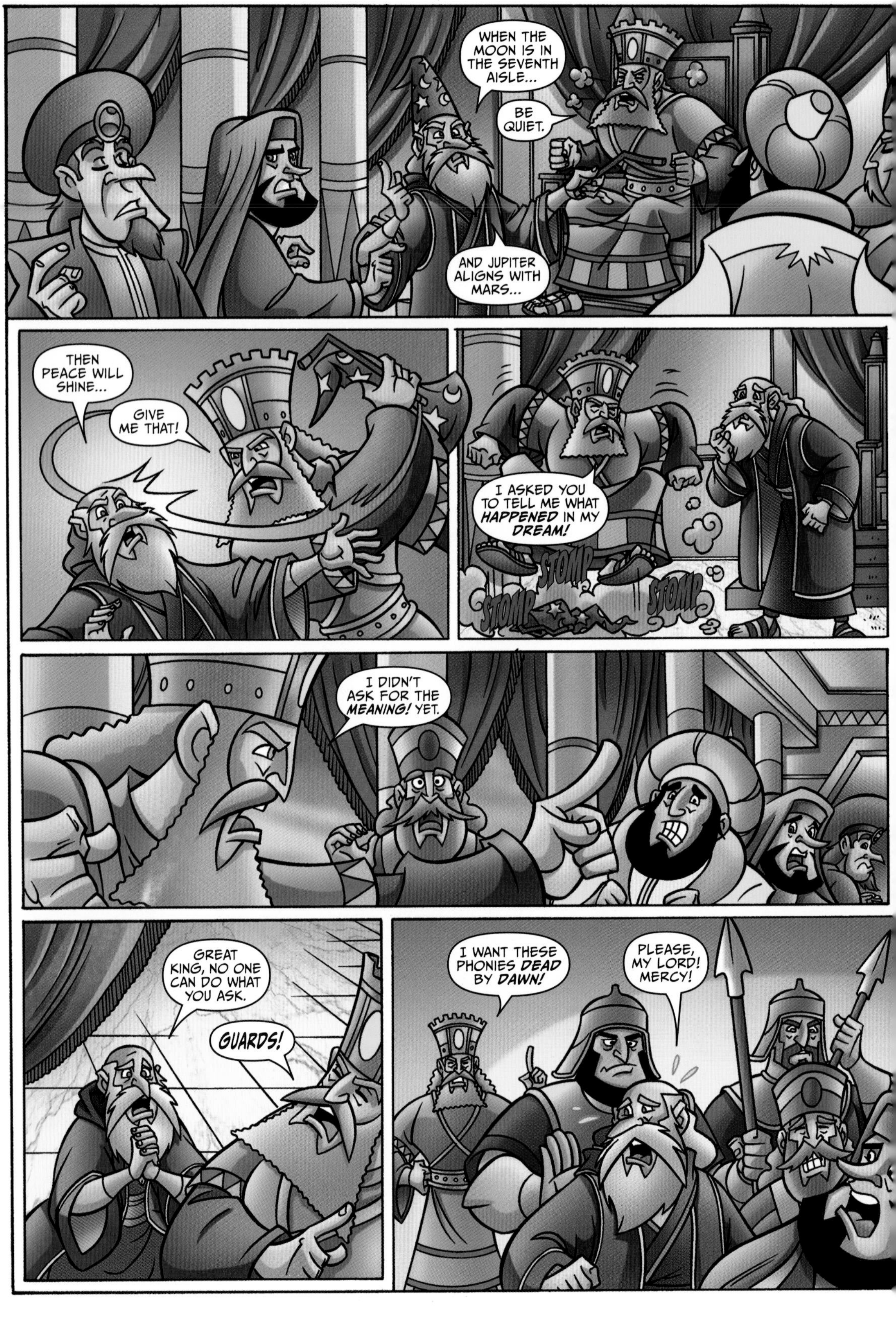
WHEN THE MOON IS IN THE SEVENTH AISLE...
BE QUIET.
AND JUPITER ALIGNS WITH MARS...
THEN PEACE WILL SHINE...
GIVE ME THAT!
I ASKED YOU TO TELL ME WHAT HAPPENED IN MY DREAM!
STOMP
STOMP
STOMP
I DIDN'T ASK FOR THE MEANING! YET.
GREAT KING, NO ONE CAN DO WHAT YOU ASK.
GUARDS!
I WANT THESE PHONIES DEAD BY DAWN!
PLEASE, MY LORD! MERCY!

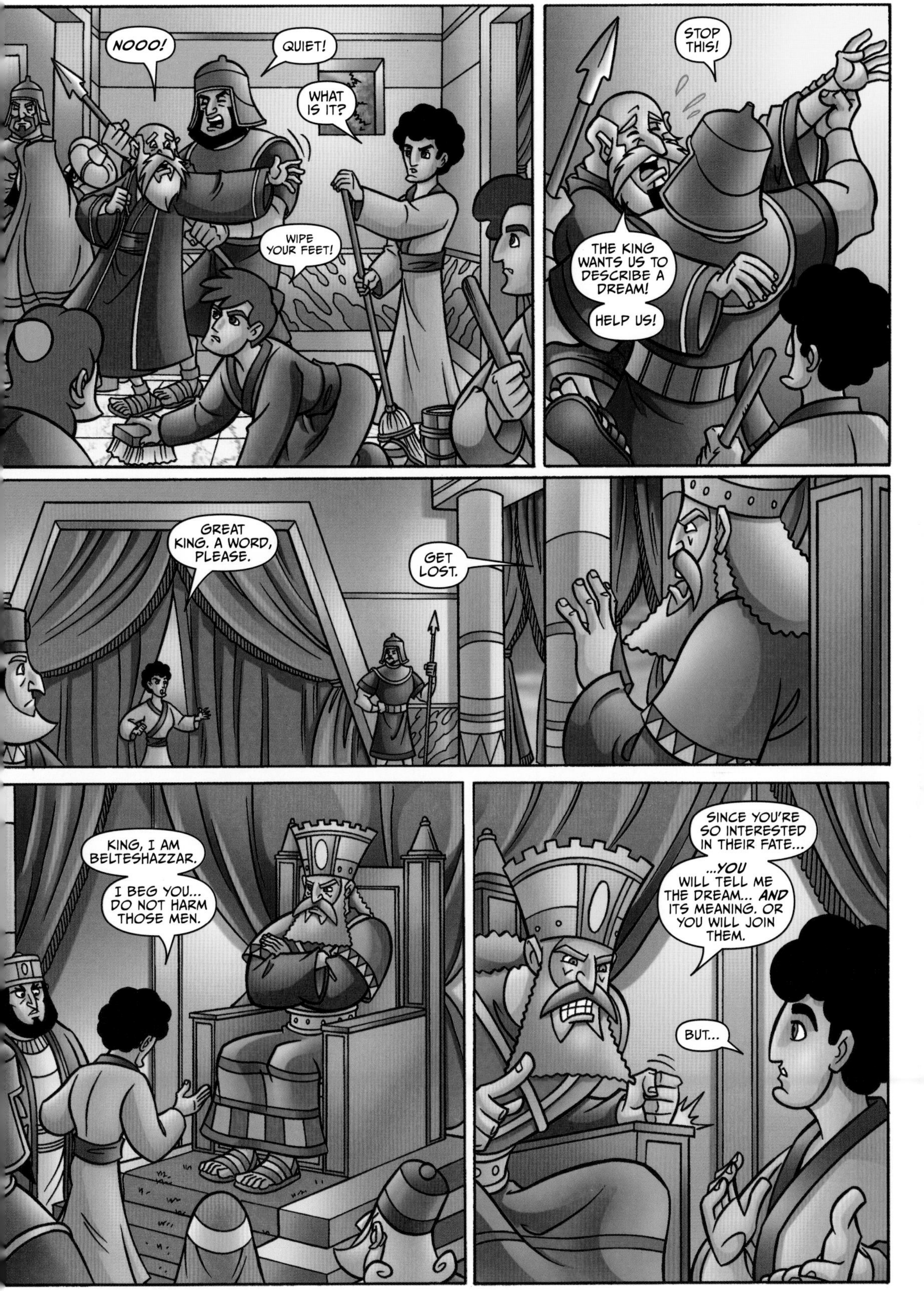
NOOO!
QUIET!
WHAT IS IT?
WIPE YOUR FEET!
STOP THIS!
THE KING WANTS US TO DESCRIBE A DREAM!
HELP US!
GREAT KING. A WORD, PLEASE.
GET LOST.
KING, I AM BELTESHAZZAR.
I BEG YOU... DO NOT HARM THOSE MEN.
SINCE YOU'RE SO INTERESTED IN THEIR FATE...
...YOU WILL TELL ME THE DREAM... AND ITS MEANING. OR YOU WILL JOIN THEM.
BUT...

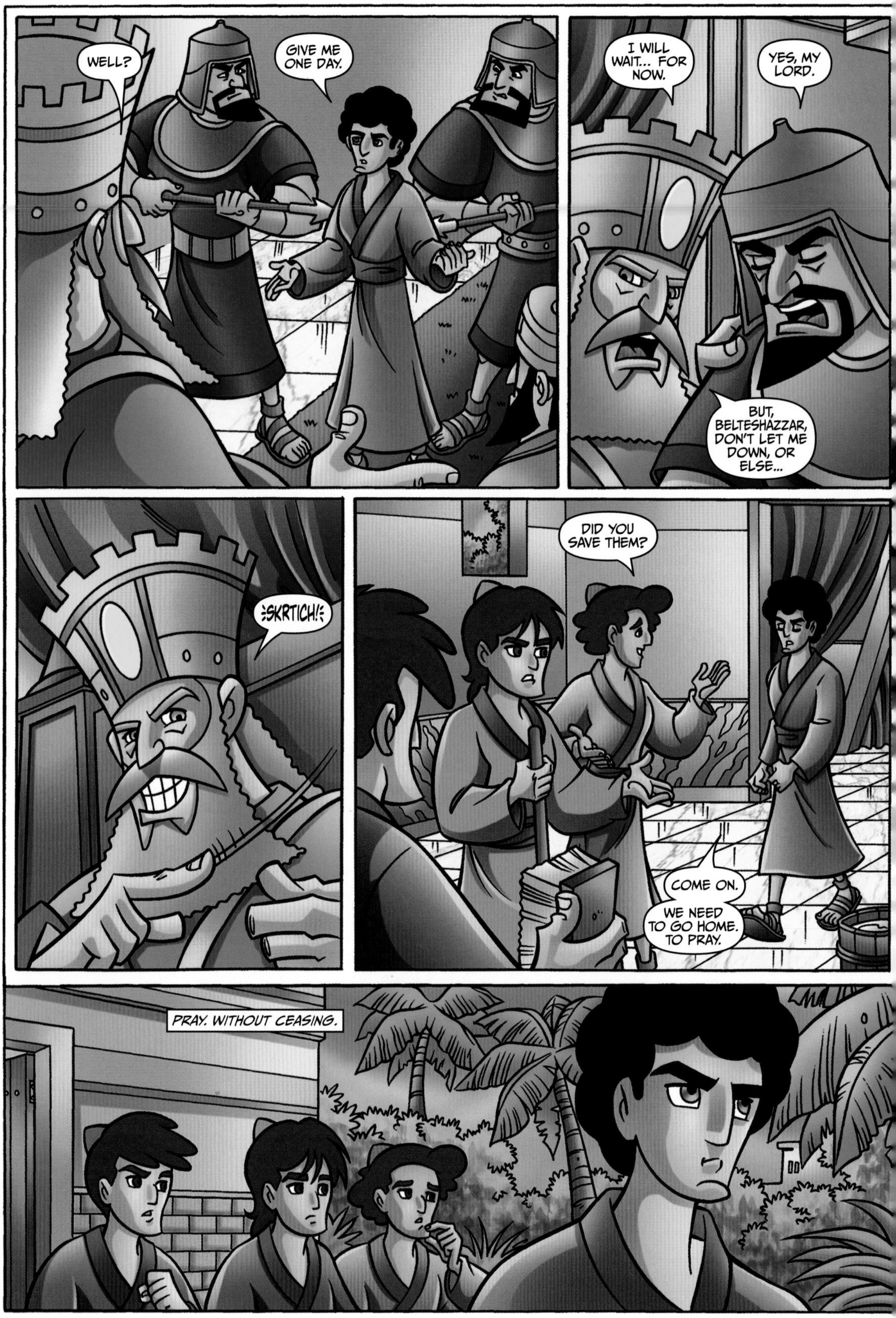
WELL?
GIVE ME ONE DAY.
I WILL WAIT... FOR NOW.
YES, MY LORD.
BUT, BELTESHAZZAR, DON'T LET ME DOWN, OR ELSE...
SKRTICH!
DID YOU SAVE THEM?
COME ON.
WE NEED TO GO HOME. TO PRAY.
PRAY. WITHOUT CEASING.

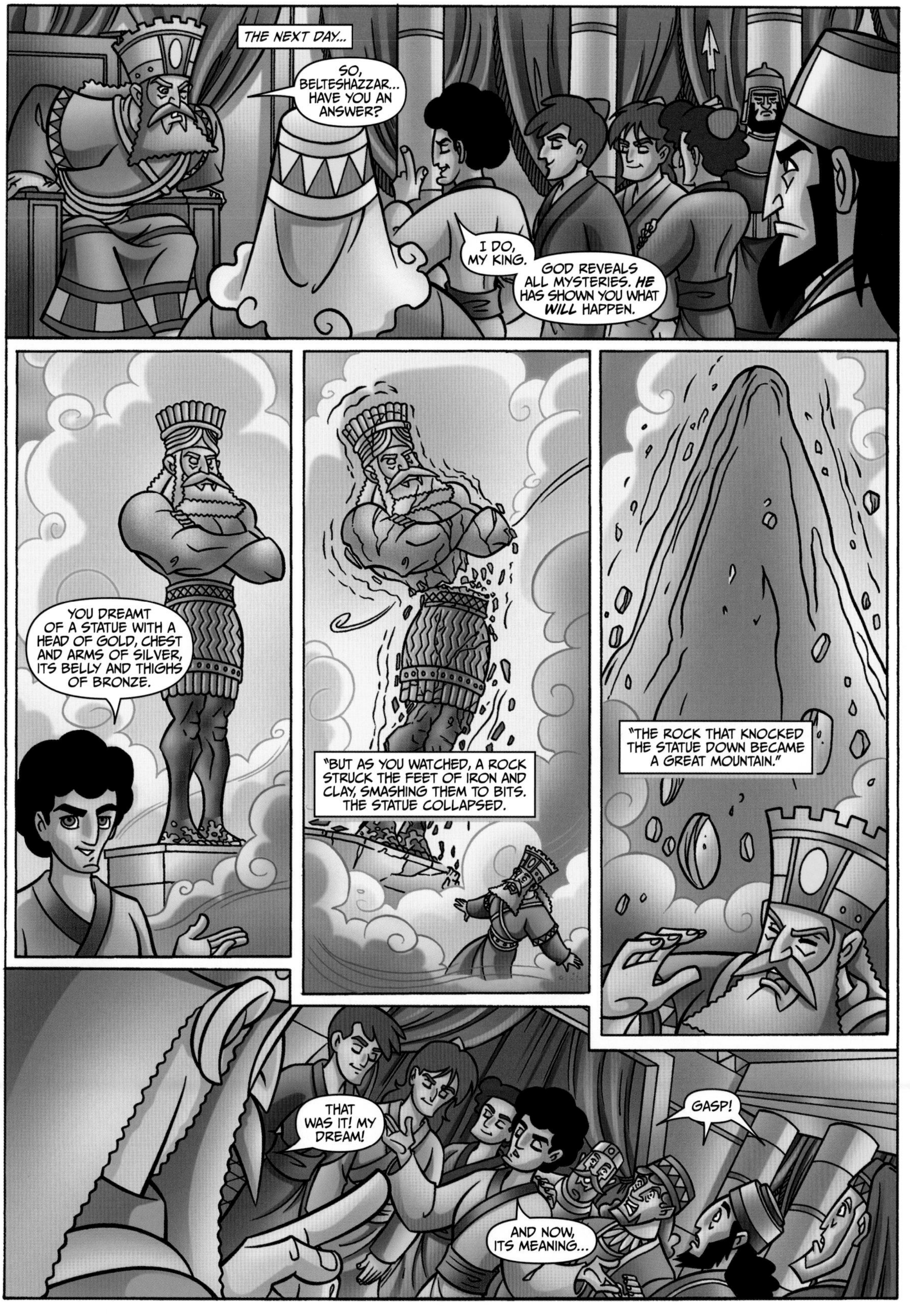
THE NEXT DAY...
SO, BELTESHAZZAR... HAVE YOU AN ANSWER?
I DO, MY KING.
GOD REVEALS ALL MYSTERIES. *HE* HAS SHOWN YOU WHAT *WILL* HAPPEN.
YOU DREAMT OF A STATUE WITH A HEAD OF GOLD, CHEST AND ARMS OF SILVER, ITS BELLY AND THIGHS OF BRONZE.
"BUT AS YOU WATCHED, A ROCK STRUCK THE FEET OF IRON AND CLAY, SMASHING THEM TO BITS. THE STATUE COLLAPSED.
"THE ROCK THAT KNOCKED THE STATUE DOWN BECAME A GREAT MOUNTAIN."
THAT WAS IT! MY DREAM!
GASP!
AND NOW, ITS MEANING...

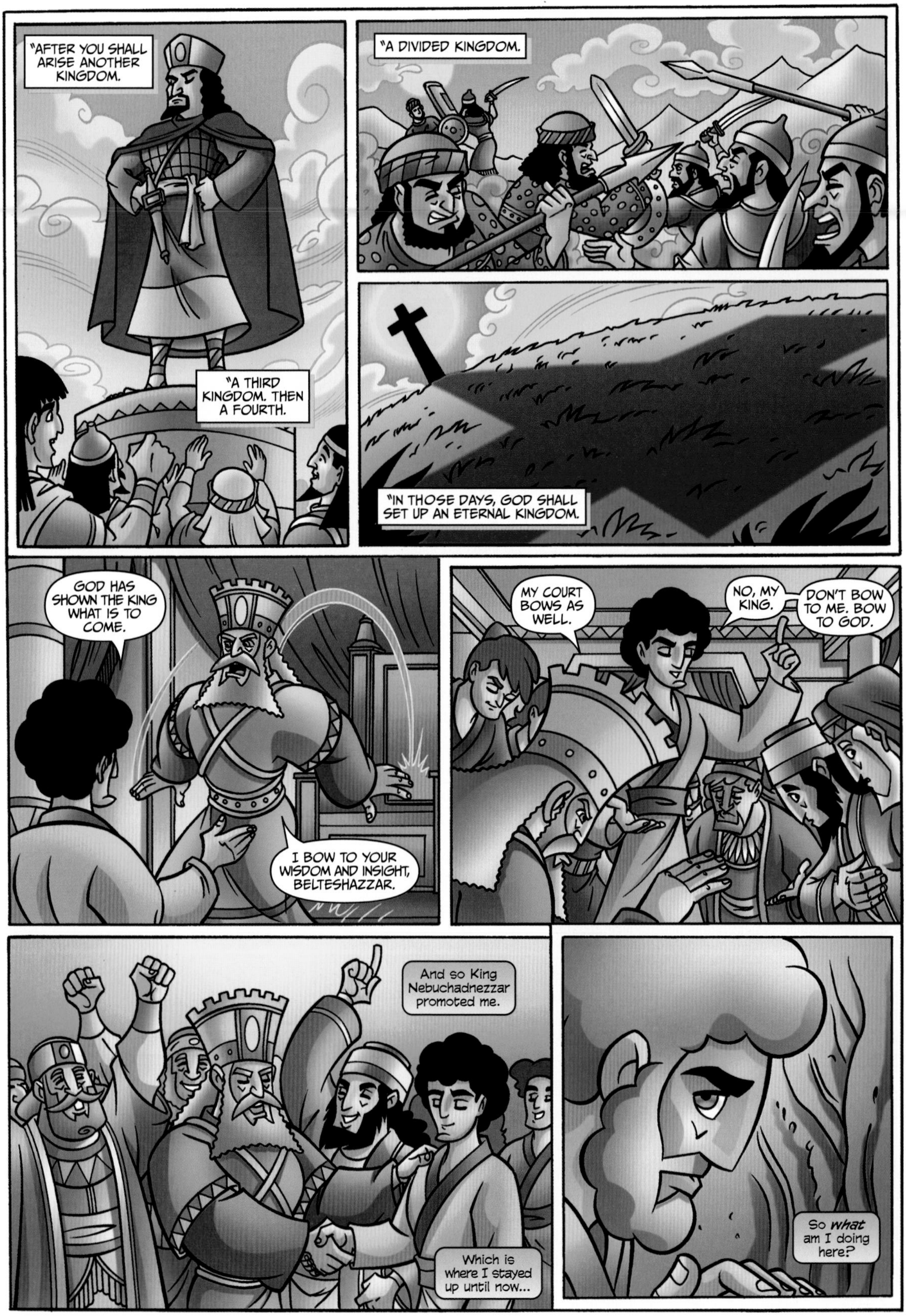
"AFTER YOU SHALL ARISE ANOTHER KINGDOM.
"A THIRD KINGDOM. THEN A FOURTH.
"A DIVIDED KINGDOM.
"IN THOSE DAYS, GOD SHALL SET UP AN ETERNAL KINGDOM.
GOD HAS SHOWN THE KING WHAT IS TO COME.
I BOW TO YOUR WISDOM AND INSIGHT, BELTESHAZZAR.
MY COURT BOWS AS WELL.
NO, MY KING.
DON'T BOW TO ME. BOW TO GOD.
And so King Nebuchadnezzar promoted me.
Which is where I stayed up until now...
So *what* am I doing here?

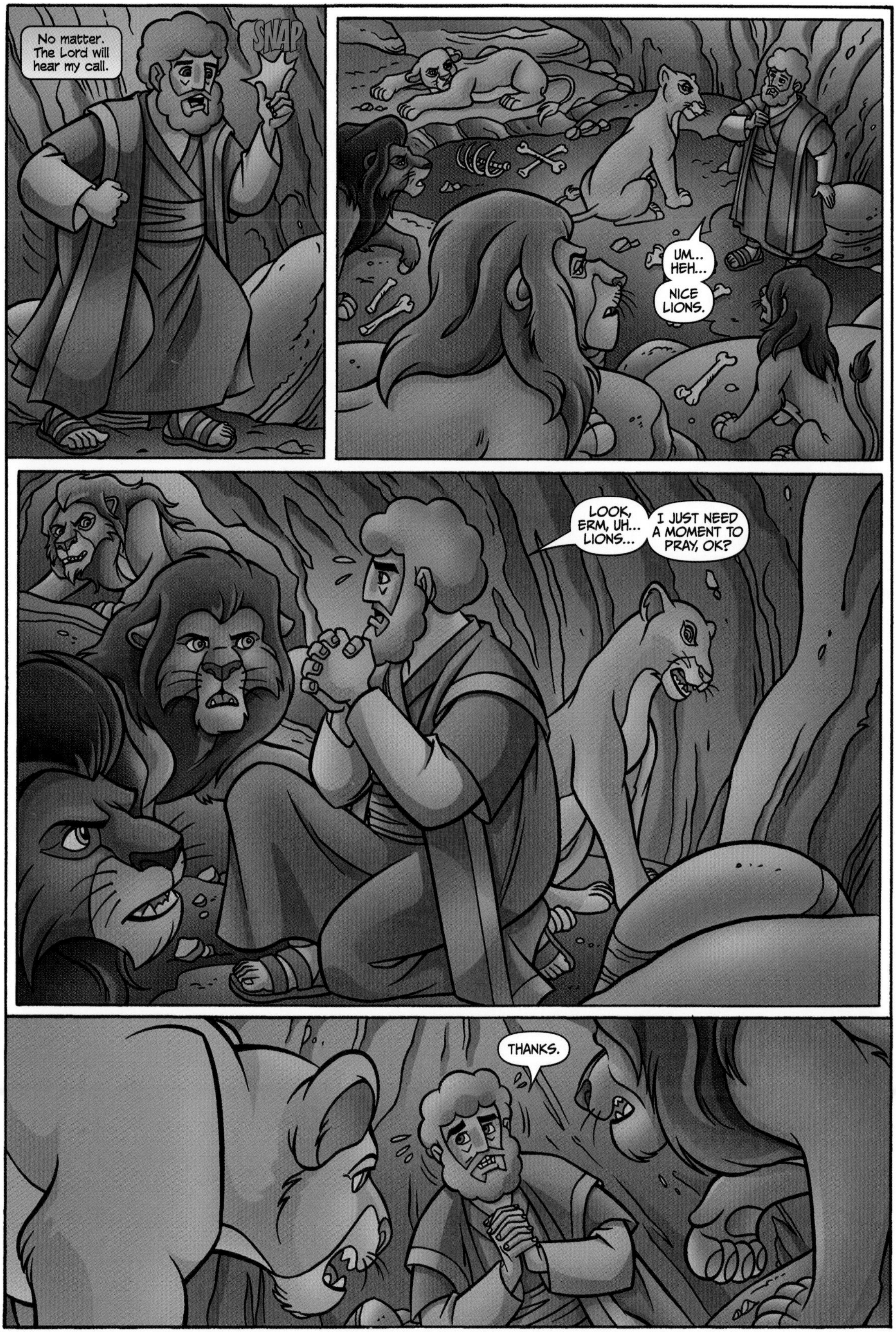
No matter. The Lord will hear my call.
SNAP
UM... HEH...
NICE LIONS.
LOOK, ERM, UH... LIONS...
I JUST NEED A MOMENT TO PRAY, OK?
THANKS.

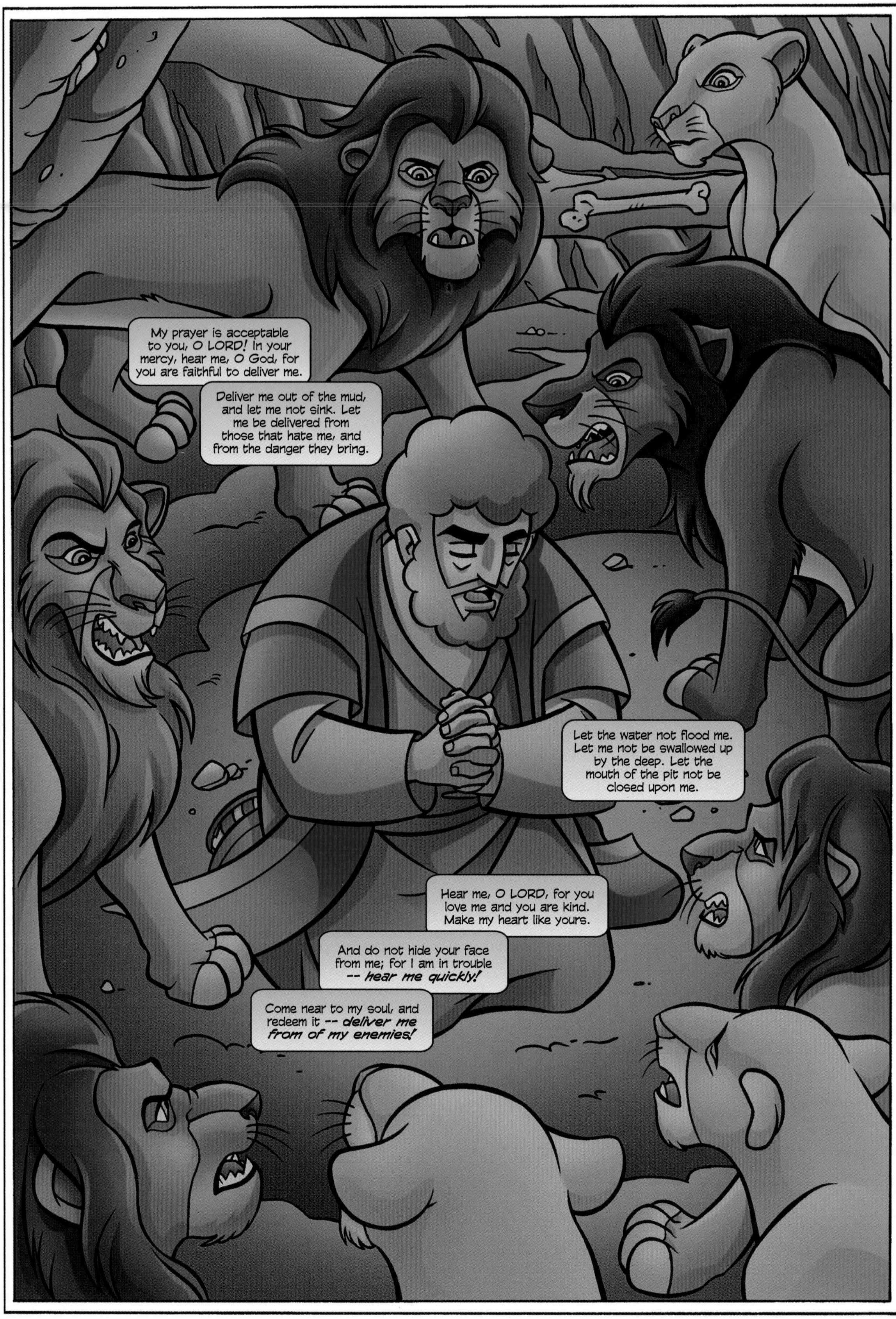
My prayer is acceptable to you, O LORD! In your mercy, hear me, O God, for you are faithful to deliver me.
Deliver me out of the mud, and let me not sink. Let me be delivered from those that hate me, and from the danger they bring.
Let the water not flood me. Let me not be swallowed up by the deep. Let the mouth of the pit not be closed upon me.
Hear me, O LORD, for you love me and you are kind. Make my heart like yours.
And do not hide your face from me; for I am in trouble -- *hear me quickly!*
Come near to my soul, and redeem it -- *deliver me from of my enemies!*

CHAPTER 4: THE FIERY FURNACE

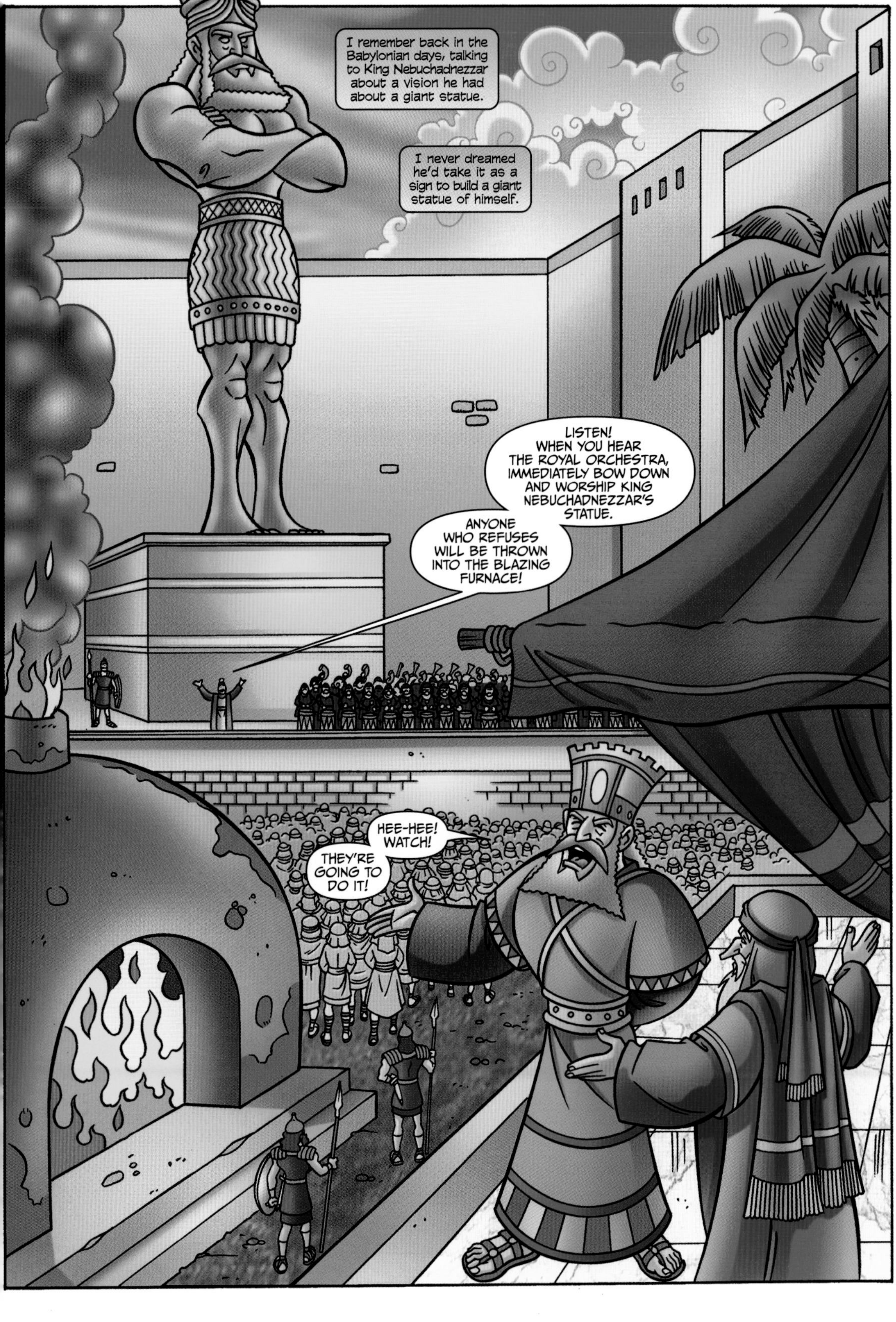
I remember back in the Babylonian days, talking to King Nebuchadnezzar about a vision he had about a giant statue.
I never dreamed he'd take it as a sign to build a giant statue of himself.
LISTEN! WHEN YOU HEAR THE ROYAL ORCHESTRA, IMMEDIATELY BOW DOWN AND WORSHIP KING NEBUCHADNEZZAR'S STATUE.
ANYONE WHO REFUSES WILL BE THROWN INTO THE BLAZING FURNACE!
HEE-HEE! WATCH!
THEY'RE GOING TO DO IT!

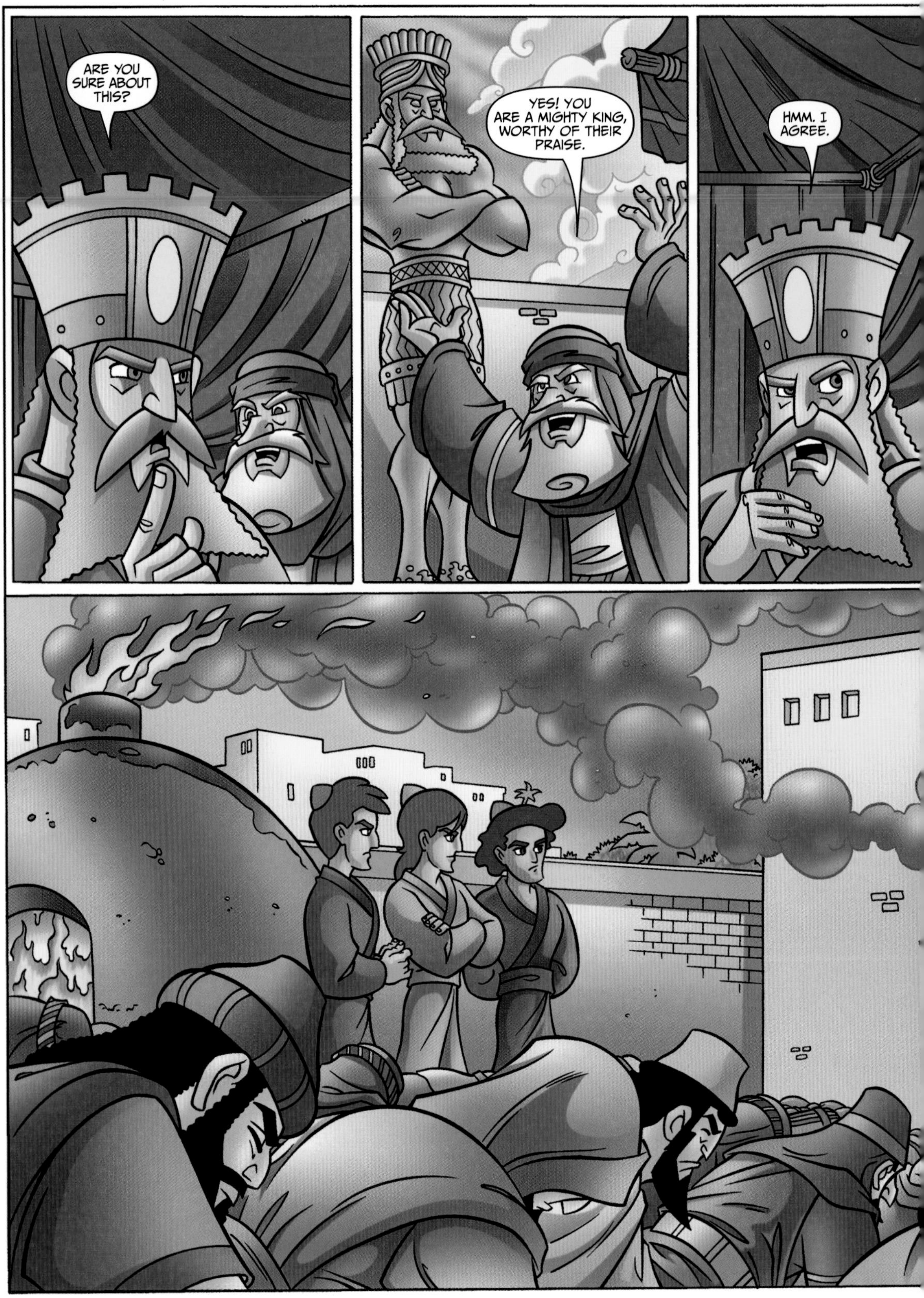
ARE YOU SURE ABOUT THIS?
YES! YOU ARE A MIGHTY KING, WORTHY OF THEIR PRAISE.
HMM. I AGREE.

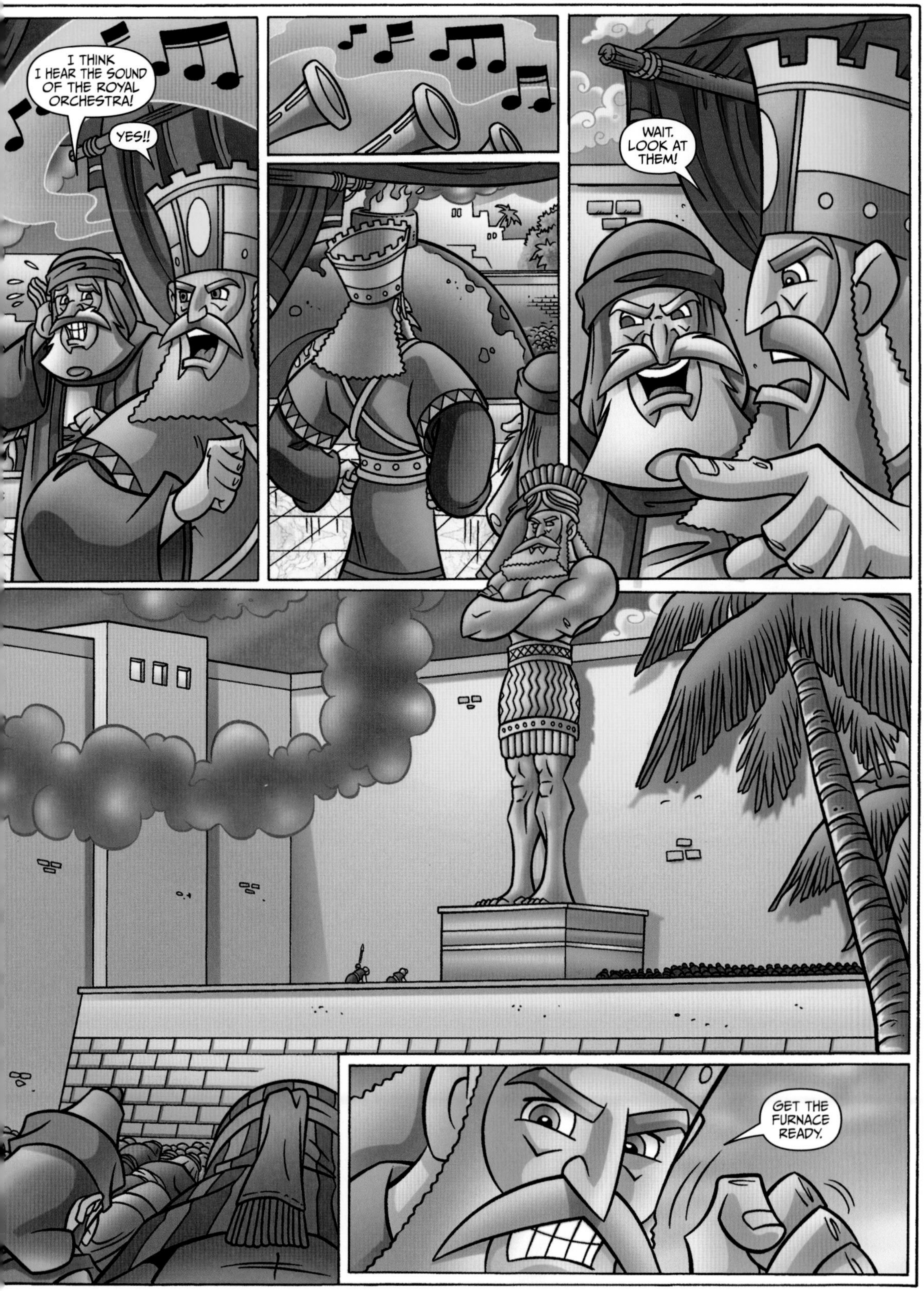
I THINK I HEAR THE SOUND OF THE ROYAL ORCHESTRA!
YES!!
WAIT. LOOK AT THEM!
GET THE FURNACE READY.

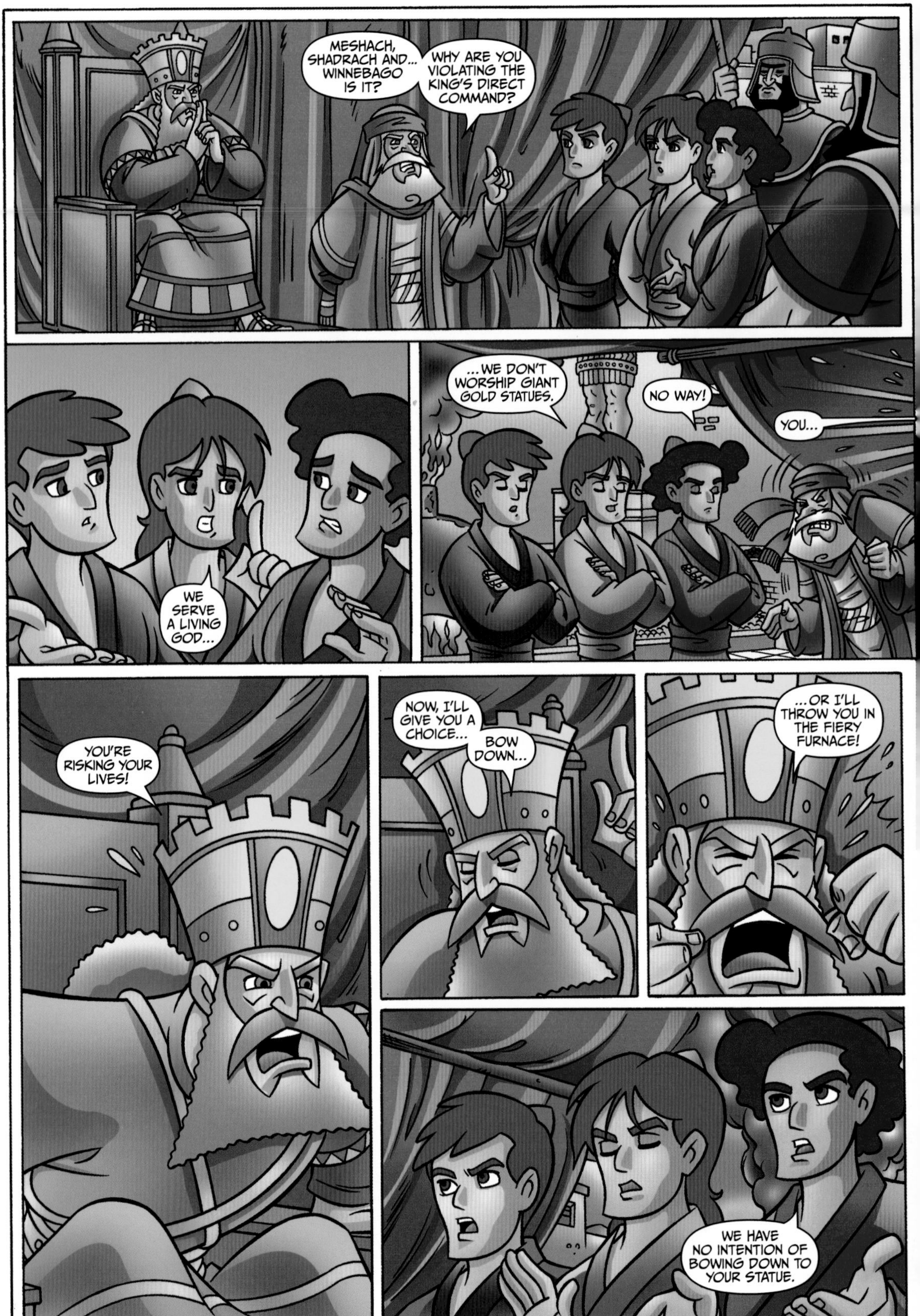
MESHACH, SHADRACH AND... WINNEBAGO IS IT?
WHY ARE YOU VIOLATING THE KING'S DIRECT COMMAND?
WE SERVE A LIVING GOD...
...WE DON'T WORSHIP GIANT GOLD STATUES.
NO WAY!
YOU...
YOU'RE RISKING YOUR LIVES!
NOW, I'LL GIVE YOU A CHOICE...
BOW DOWN...
...OR I'LL THROW YOU IN THE FIERY FURNACE!
WE HAVE NO INTENTION OF BOWING DOWN TO YOUR STATUE.

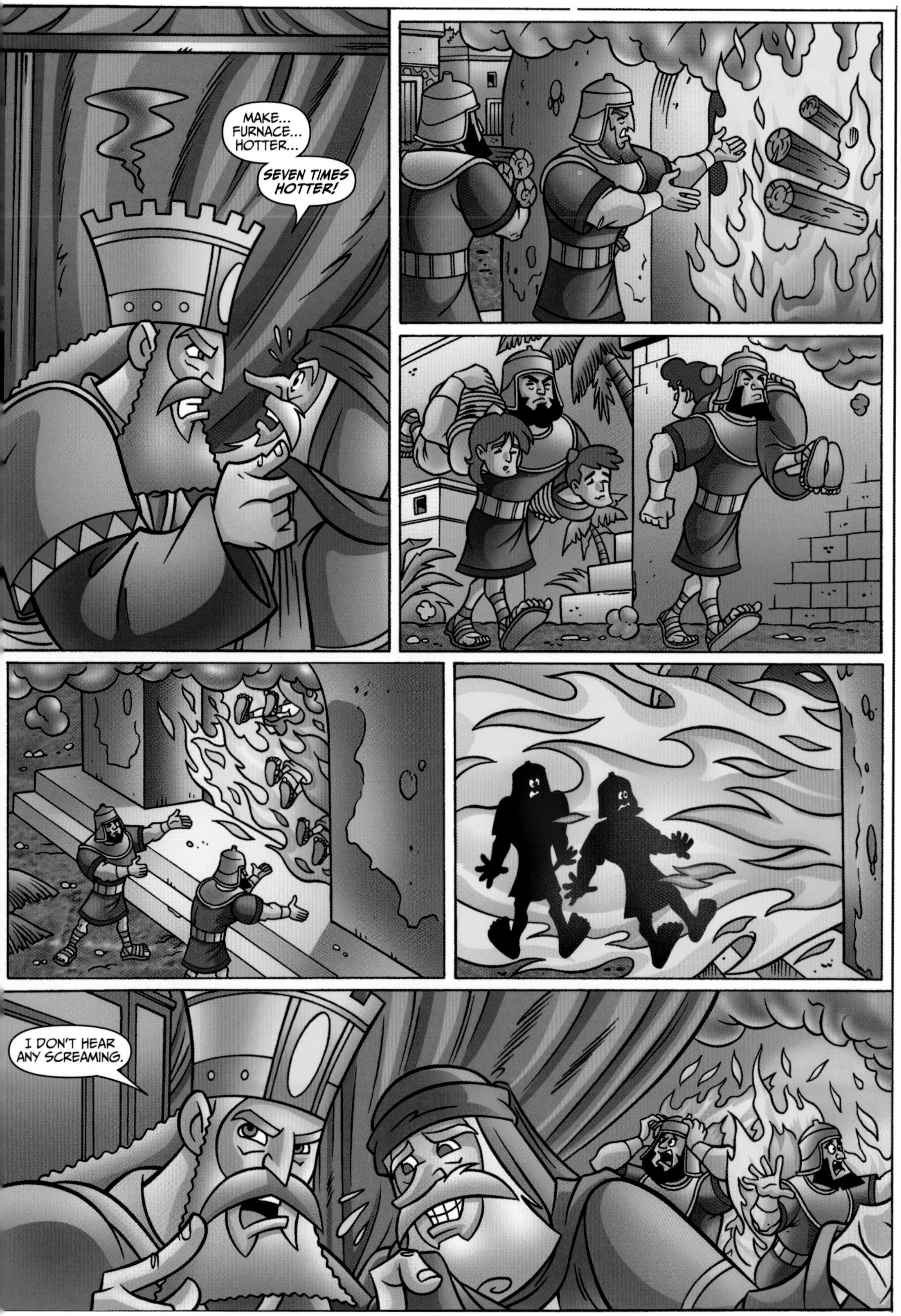
MAKE... FURNACE... HOTTER...
SEVEN TIMES HOTTER!
I DON'T HEAR ANY SCREAMING.

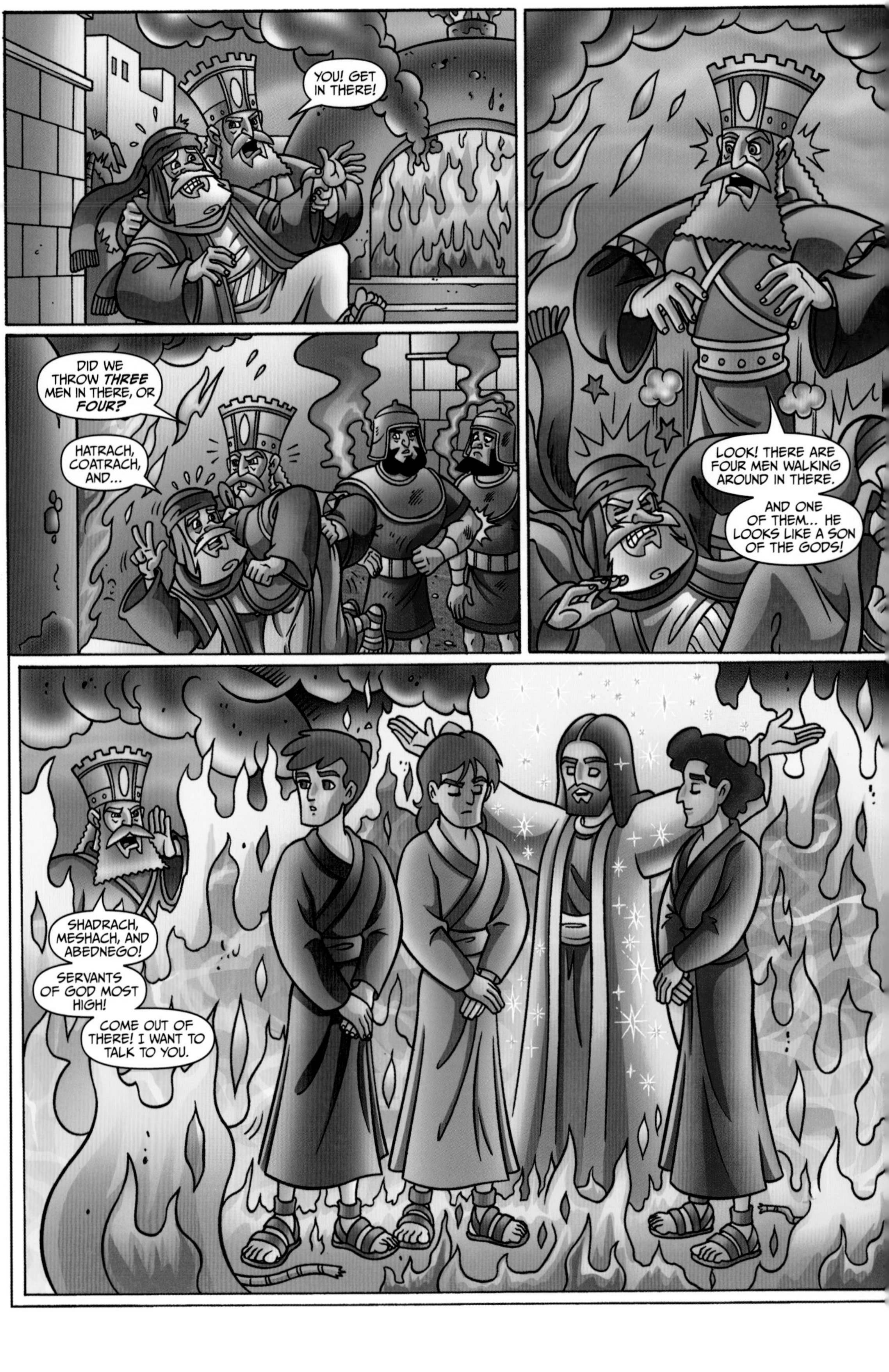
YOU! GET IN THERE!
DID WE THROW *THREE* MEN IN THERE, OR *FOUR?*
HATRACH, COATRACH, AND...
LOOK! THERE ARE FOUR MEN WALKING AROUND IN THERE.
AND ONE OF THEM... HE LOOKS LIKE A SON OF THE GODS!
SHADRACH, MESHACH, AND ABEDNEGO!
SERVANTS OF GOD MOST HIGH!
COME OUT OF THERE! I WANT TO TALK TO YOU.

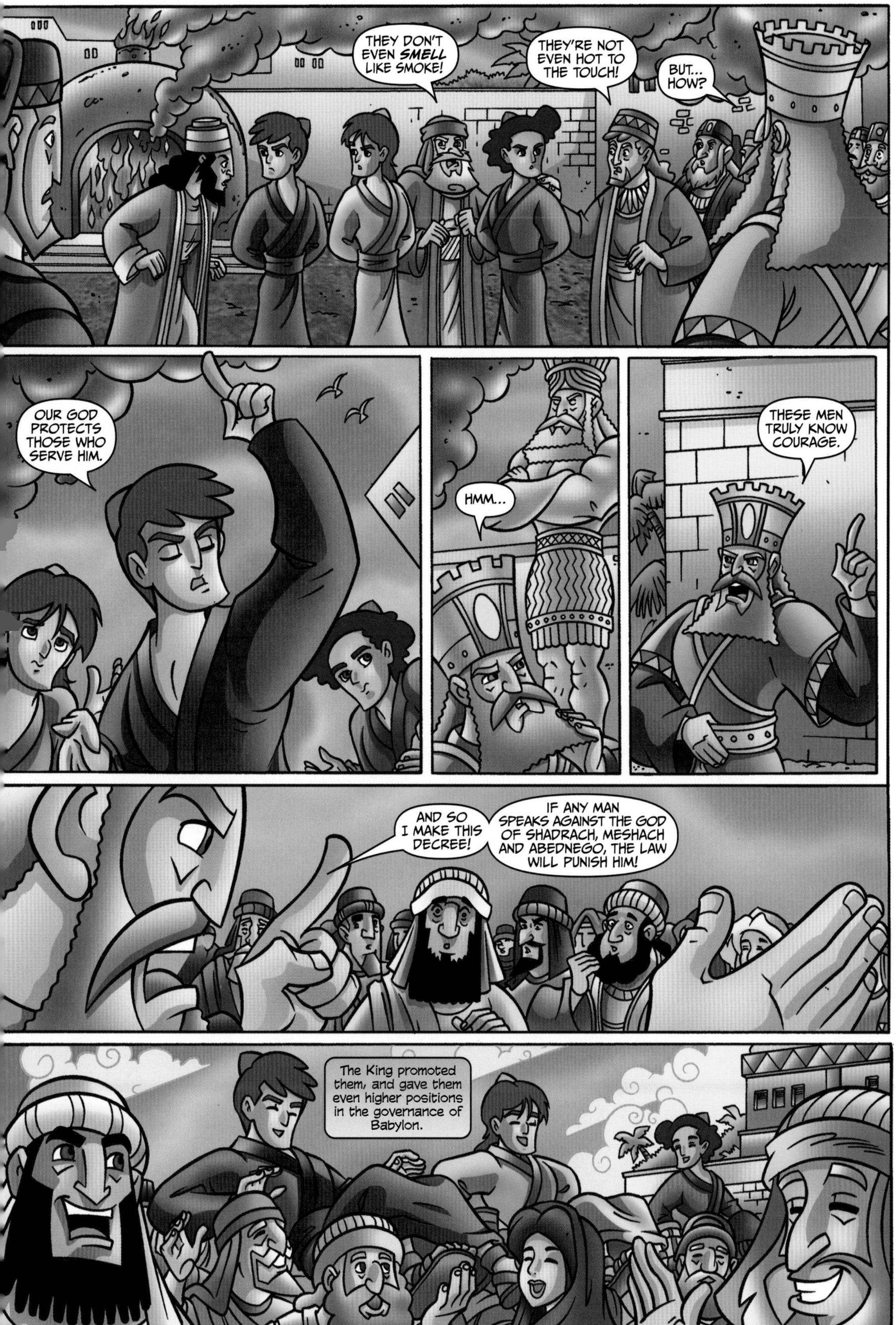
THEY DON'T EVEN SMELL LIKE SMOKE!
THEY'RE NOT EVEN HOT TO THE TOUCH!
BUT... HOW?
OUR GOD PROTECTS THOSE WHO SERVE HIM.
HMM...
THESE MEN TRULY KNOW COURAGE.
AND SO I MAKE THIS DECREE!
IF ANY MAN SPEAKS AGAINST THE GOD OF SHADRACH, MESHACH AND ABEDNEGO, THE LAW WILL PUNISH HIM!
The King promoted them, and gave them even higher positions in the governance of Babylon.

CHAPTER 5: THE MADNESS OF THE KING

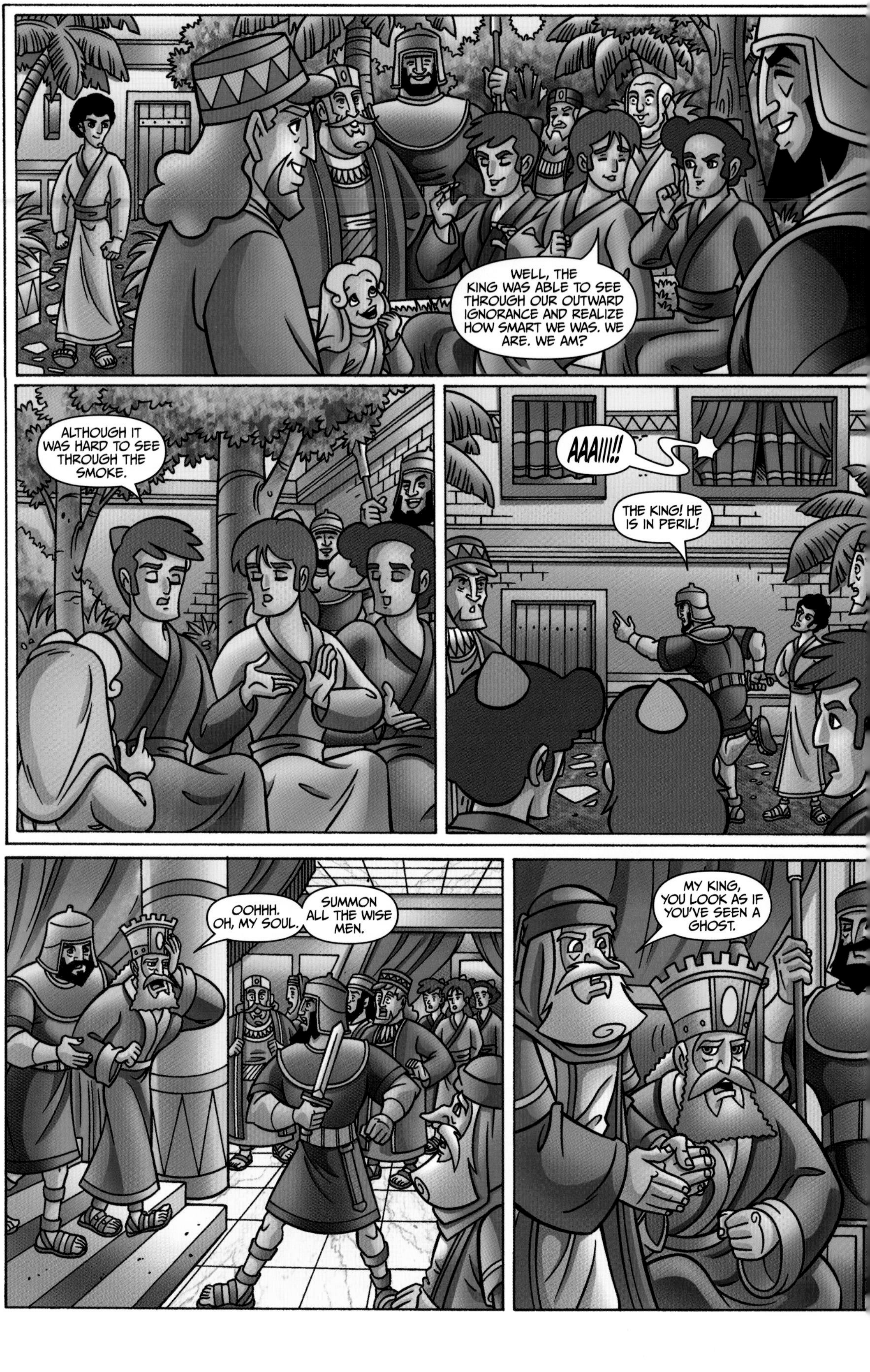
WELL, THE KING WAS ABLE TO SEE THROUGH OUR OUTWARD IGNORANCE AND REALIZE HOW SMART WE WAS. WE ARE. WE AM?
ALTHOUGH IT WAS HARD TO SEE THROUGH THE SMOKE.
AAAII!!!
THE KING! HE IS IN PERIL!
OOHHH. OH, MY SOUL.
SUMMON ALL THE WISE MEN.
MY KING, YOU LOOK AS IF YOU'VE SEEN A GHOST.

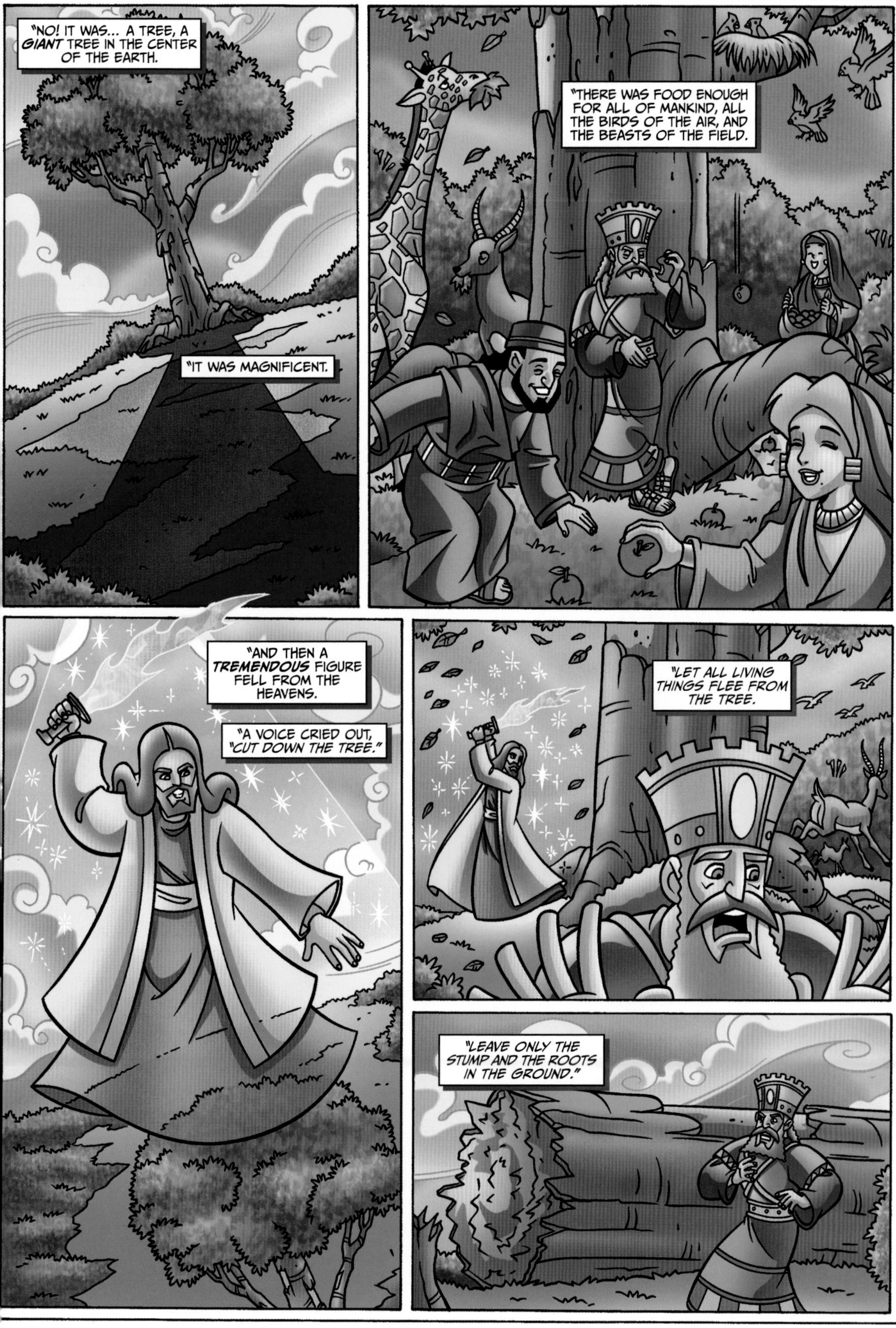
"NO! IT WAS... A TREE, A *GIANT* TREE IN THE CENTER OF THE EARTH.
"IT WAS MAGNIFICENT.
"THERE WAS FOOD ENOUGH FOR ALL OF MANKIND, ALL THE BIRDS OF THE AIR, AND THE BEASTS OF THE FIELD.
"AND THEN A *TREMENDOUS* FIGURE FELL FROM THE HEAVENS.
"A VOICE CRIED OUT, *"CUT DOWN THE TREE."*
"LET ALL LIVING THINGS FLEE FROM THE TREE.
"LEAVE ONLY THE STUMP AND THE ROOTS IN THE GROUND."

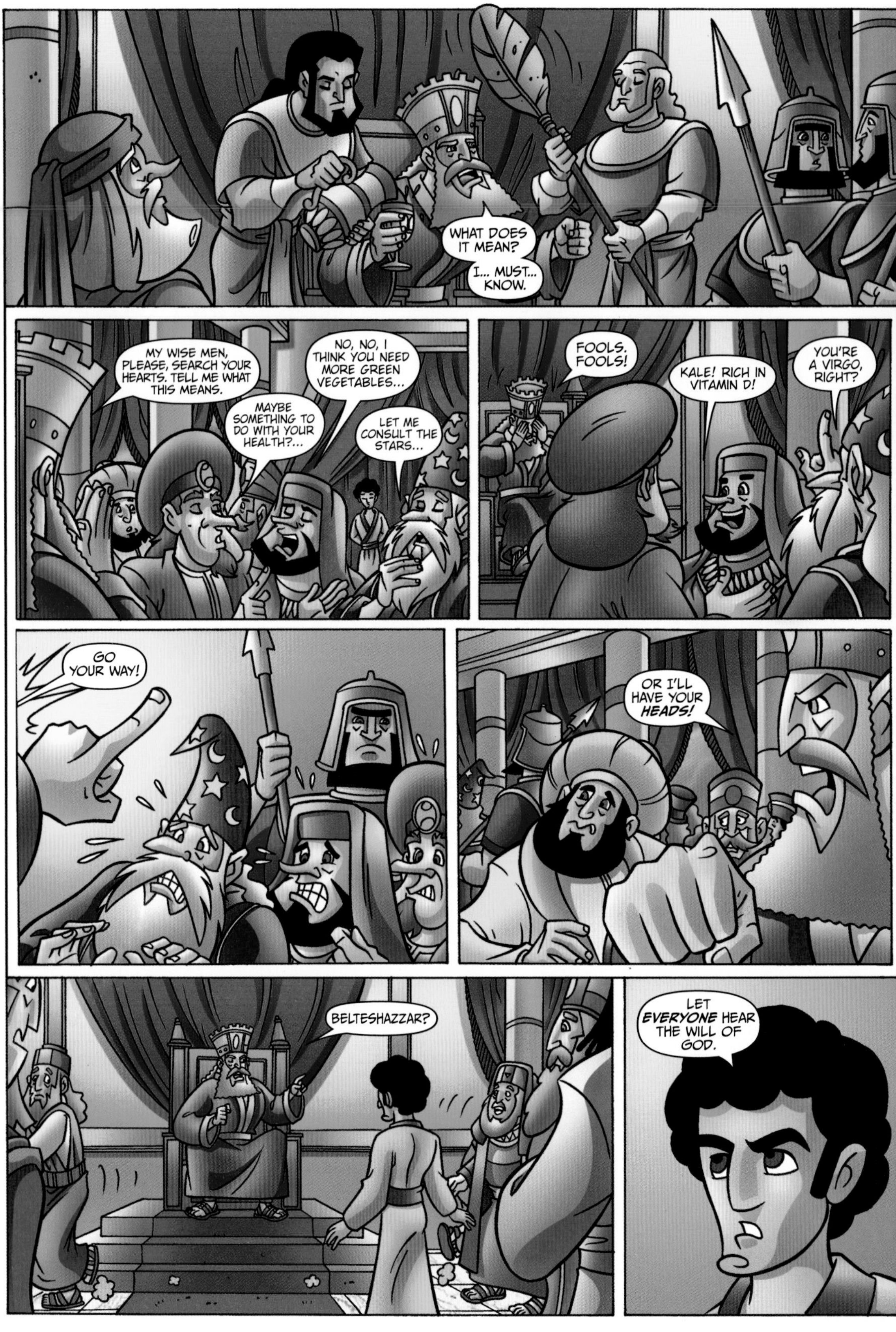
WHAT DOES IT MEAN?
I... MUST... KNOW.
MY WISE MEN, PLEASE, SEARCH YOUR HEARTS. TELL ME WHAT THIS MEANS.
MAYBE SOMETHING TO DO WITH YOUR HEALTH?...
NO, NO, I THINK YOU NEED MORE GREEN VEGETABLES...
LET ME CONSULT THE STARS...
FOOLS. FOOLS!
KALE! RICH IN VITAMIN D!
YOU'RE A VIRGO, RIGHT?
GO YOUR WAY!
OR I'LL HAVE YOUR HEADS!
BELTESHAZZAR?
LET EVERYONE HEAR THE WILL OF GOD.

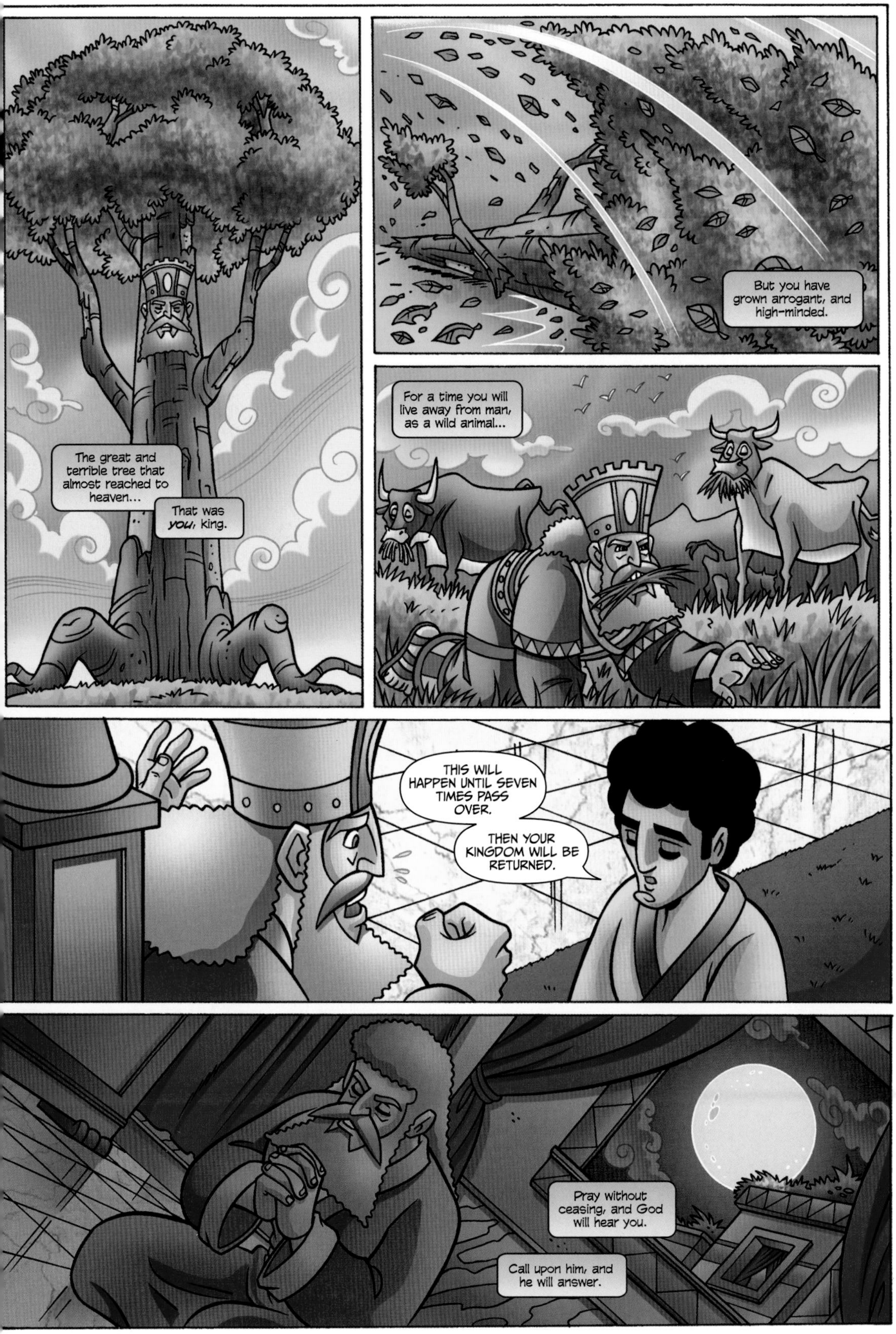
The great and terrible tree that almost reached to heaven...
That was *you*, king.
But you have grown arrogant, and high-minded.
For a time you will live away from man, as a wild animal...
THIS WILL HAPPEN UNTIL SEVEN TIMES PASS OVER.
THEN YOUR KINGDOM WILL BE RETURNED.
Pray without ceasing, and God will hear you.
Call upon him, and he will answer.

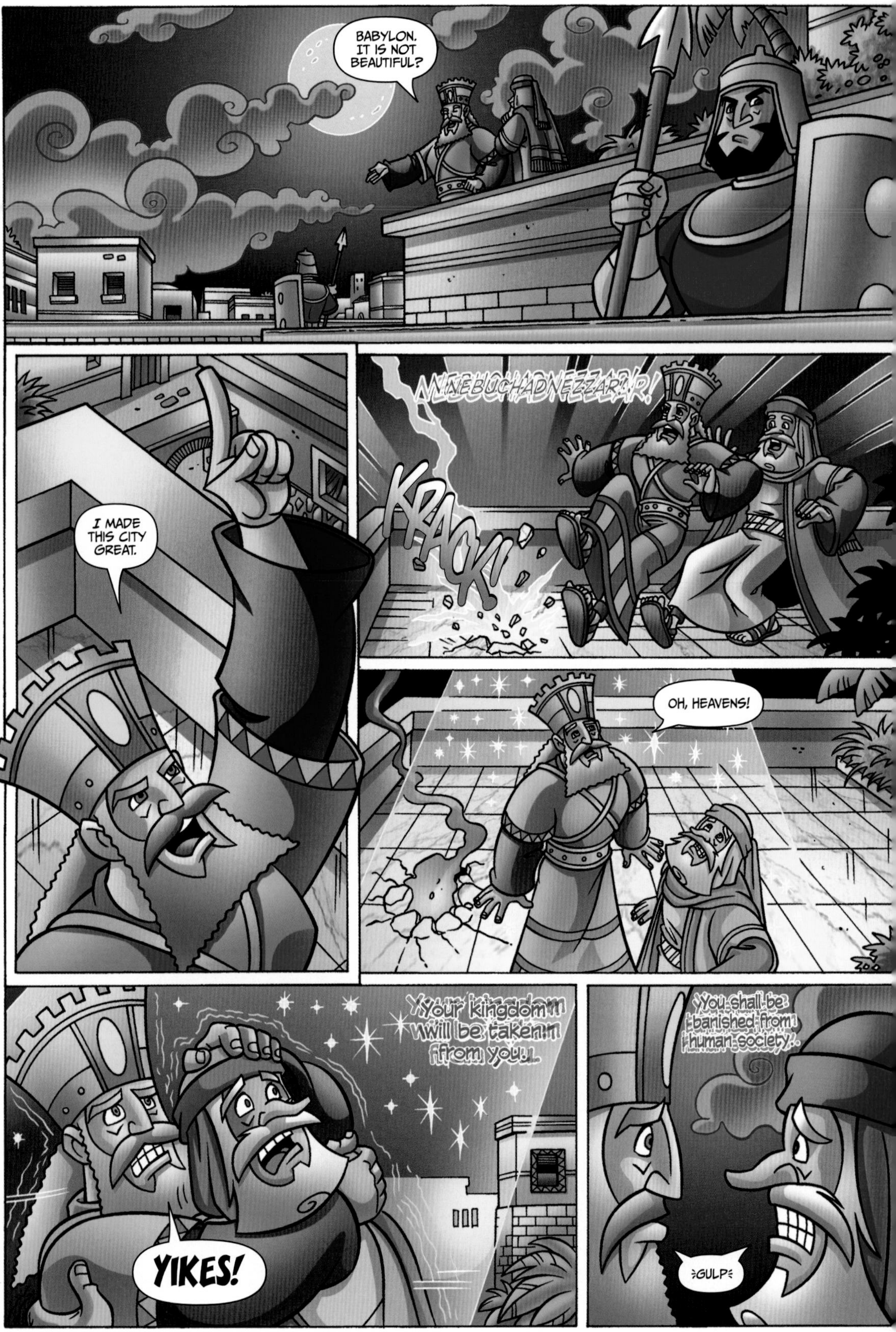
BABYLON. IT IS NOT BEAUTIFUL?
I MADE THIS CITY GREAT.
NEBUCHADNEZZAR!
KRACK!
OH, HEAVENS!
Your kingdom will be taken from you...
YIKES!
You shall be banished from human society...
GULP

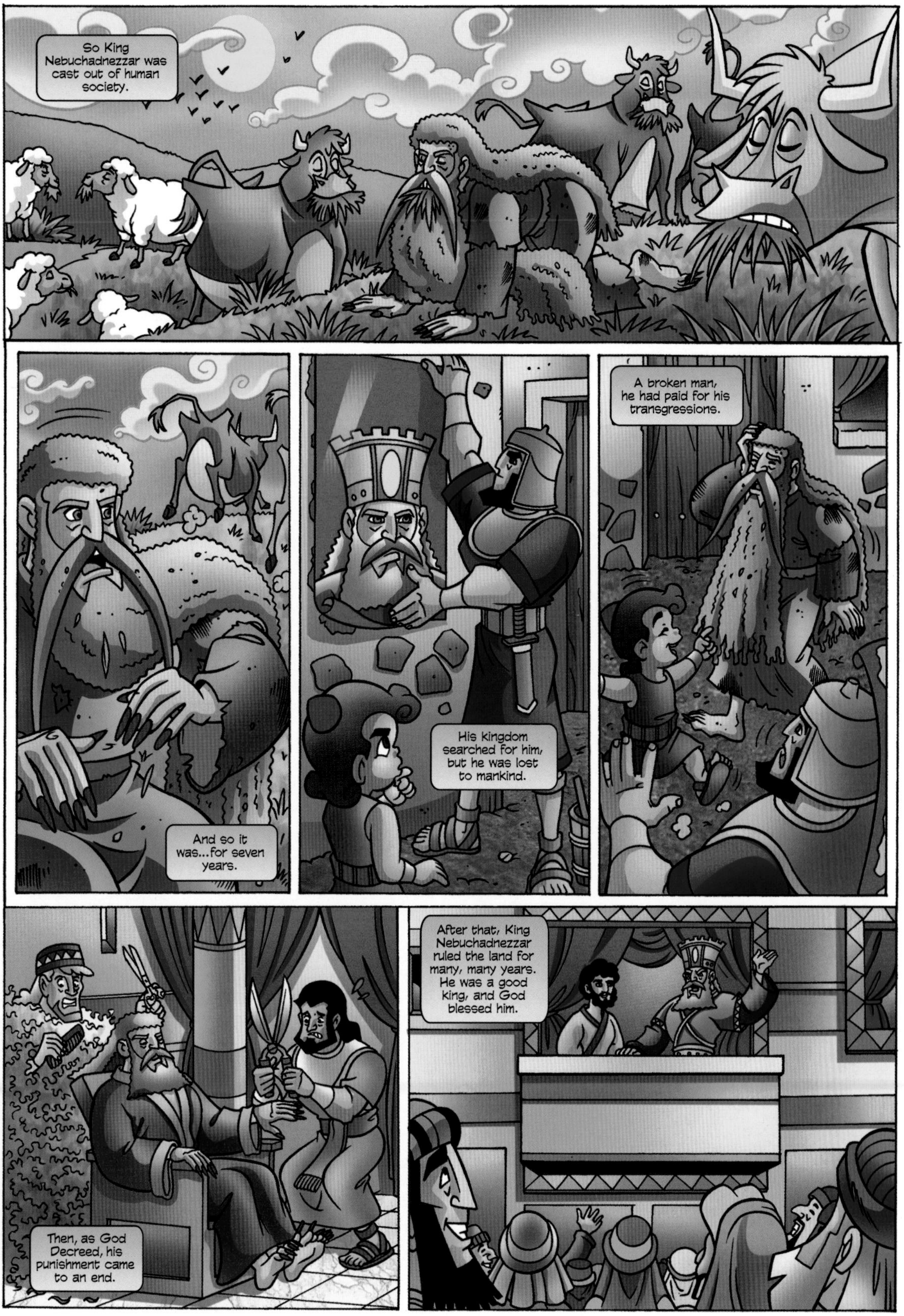

So King Nebuchadnezzar was cast out of human society.
And so it was...for seven years.
His kingdom searched for him, but he was lost to mankind.
A broken man, he had paid for his transgressions.
Then, as God Decreed, his punishment came to an end.
After that, King Nebuchadnezzar ruled the land for many, many years. He was a good king, and God blessed him.

CHAPTER 6: THE WRITING ON THE WALL

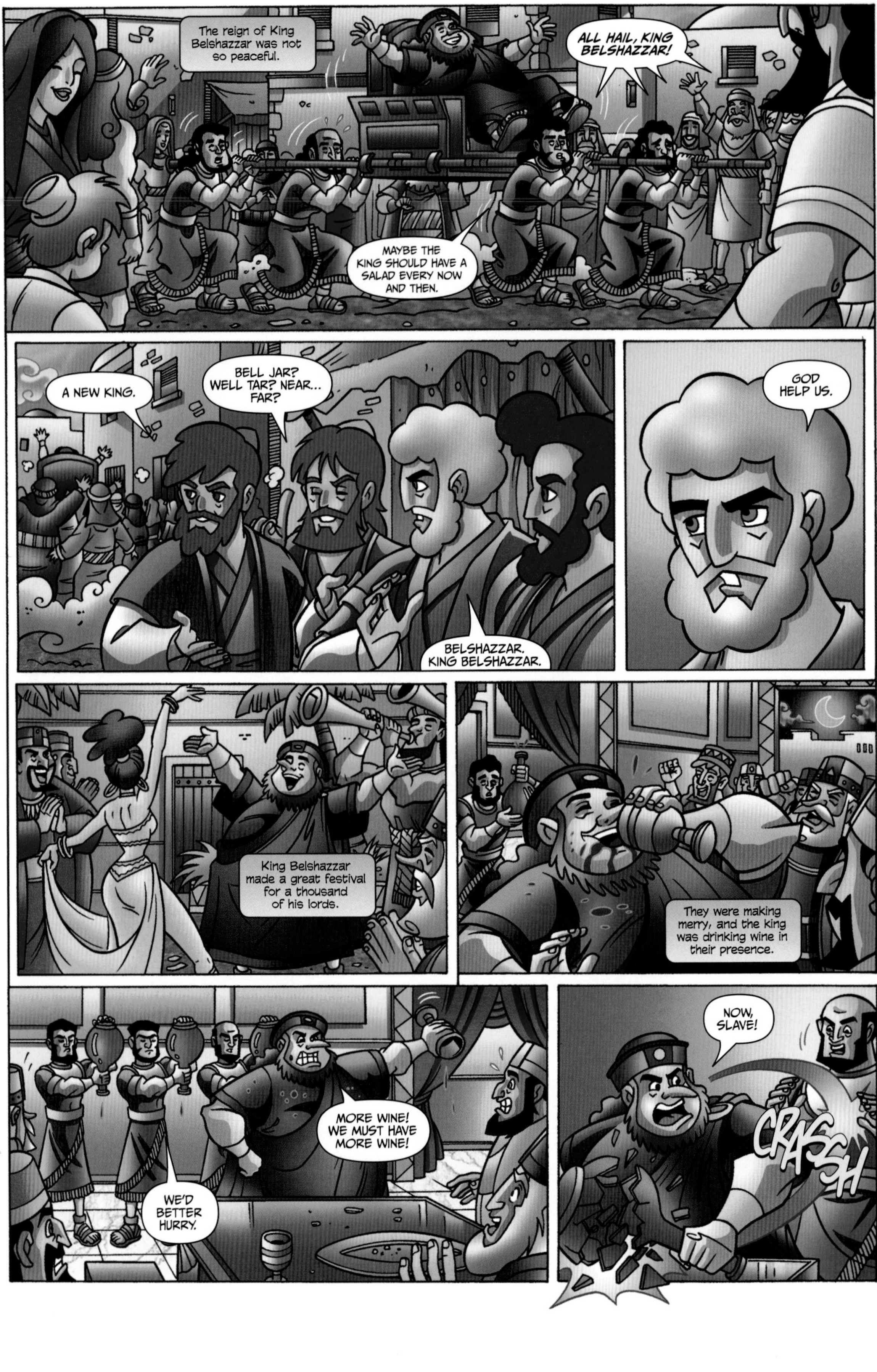

The reign of King Belshazzar was not so peaceful.
ALL HAIL, KING BELSHAZZAR!
MAYBE THE KING SHOULD HAVE A SALAD EVERY NOW AND THEN.
A NEW KING.
BELL JAR? WELL TAR? NEAR... FAR?
BELSHAZZAR. KING BELSHAZZAR.
GOD HELP US.
King Belshazzar made a great festival for a thousand of his lords.
They were making merry, and the king was drinking wine in their presence.
MORE WINE! WE MUST HAVE MORE WINE!
WE'D BETTER HURRY.
NOW, SLAVE!
CRASSH

KING, AS YOU REQUESTED, WE REMOVED THE GOLD AND SILVER WINE VESSELS FROM THE TEMPLE.

BUT THE JEWISH PEOPLE WERE VERY ANGRY.

YES!

MORE WINE, MY LORD?

GREAT KING, LOOK!

NOW THAT'S JUST RUDE.

PTOOEEEY!

מנא מנא תקל ופרסין

WHAT... WHAT IS...

BY THE GODS!

WHAT MANNER OF MAGIC...

WHAT IS THIS MYSTERY?

I DO NOT KNOW. HEAVENS!

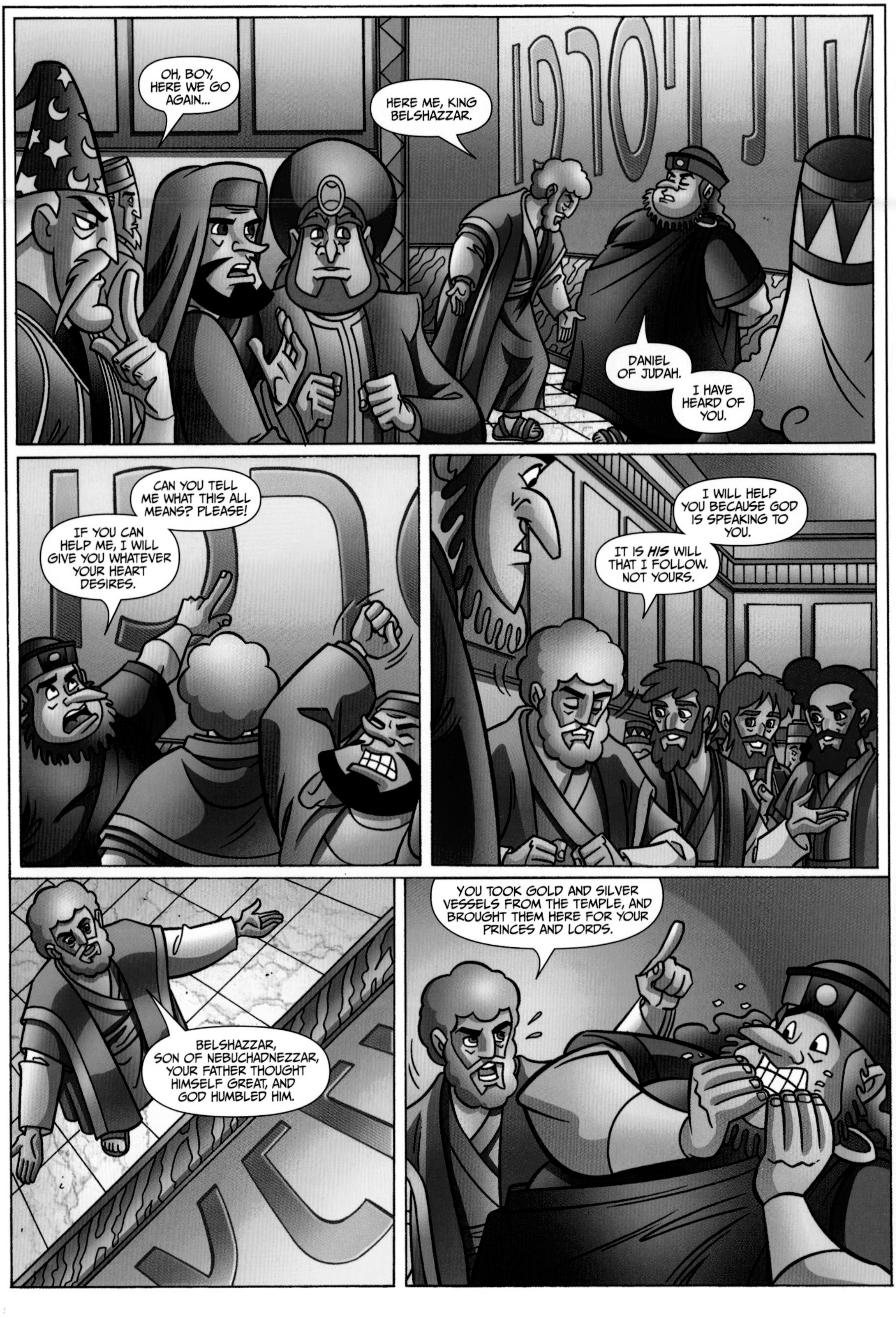
OH, BOY, HERE WE GO AGAIN...
HERE ME, KING BELSHAZZAR.
DANIEL OF JUDAH.
I HAVE HEARD OF YOU.
CAN YOU TELL ME WHAT THIS ALL MEANS? PLEASE!
IF YOU CAN HELP ME, I WILL GIVE YOU WHATEVER YOUR HEART DESIRES.
I WILL HELP YOU BECAUSE GOD IS SPEAKING TO YOU.
IT IS *HIS* WILL THAT I FOLLOW. NOT YOURS.
BELSHAZZAR, SON OF NEBUCHADNEZZAR, YOUR FATHER THOUGHT HIMSELF GREAT, AND GOD HUMBLED HIM.
YOU TOOK GOLD AND SILVER VESSELS FROM THE TEMPLE, AND BROUGHT THEM HERE FOR YOUR PRINCES AND LORDS.

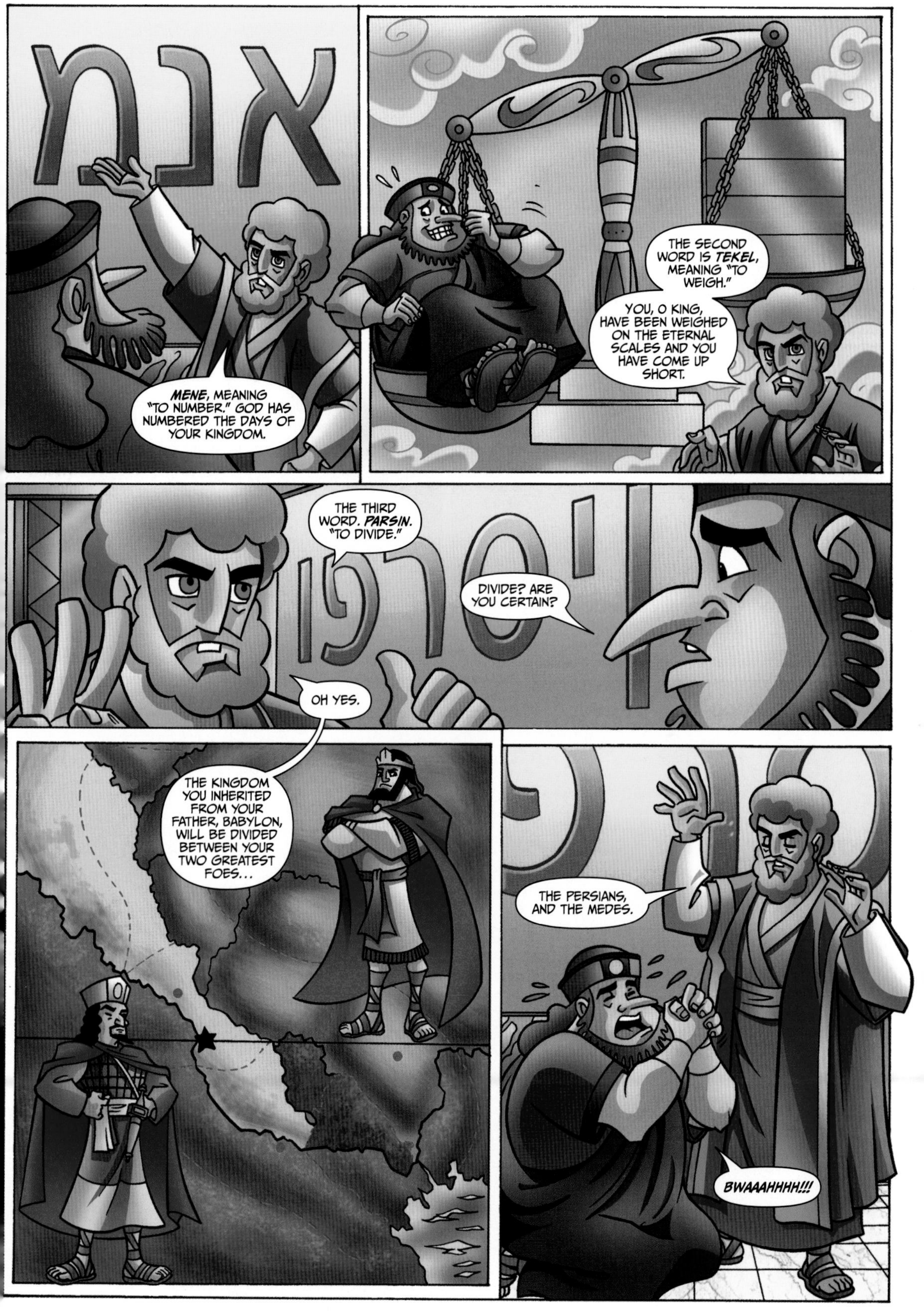
MENE, MEANING "TO NUMBER." GOD HAS NUMBERED THE DAYS OF YOUR KINGDOM.
THE SECOND WORD IS TEKEL, MEANING "TO WEIGH."
YOU, O KING, HAVE BEEN WEIGHED ON THE ETERNAL SCALES AND YOU HAVE COME UP SHORT.
THE THIRD WORD. PARSIN. "TO DIVIDE."
DIVIDE? ARE YOU CERTAIN?
OH YES.
THE KINGDOM YOU INHERITED FROM YOUR FATHER, BABYLON, WILL BE DIVIDED BETWEEN YOUR TWO GREATEST FOES...
THE PERSIANS, AND THE MEDES.
BWAAAHHHH!!!

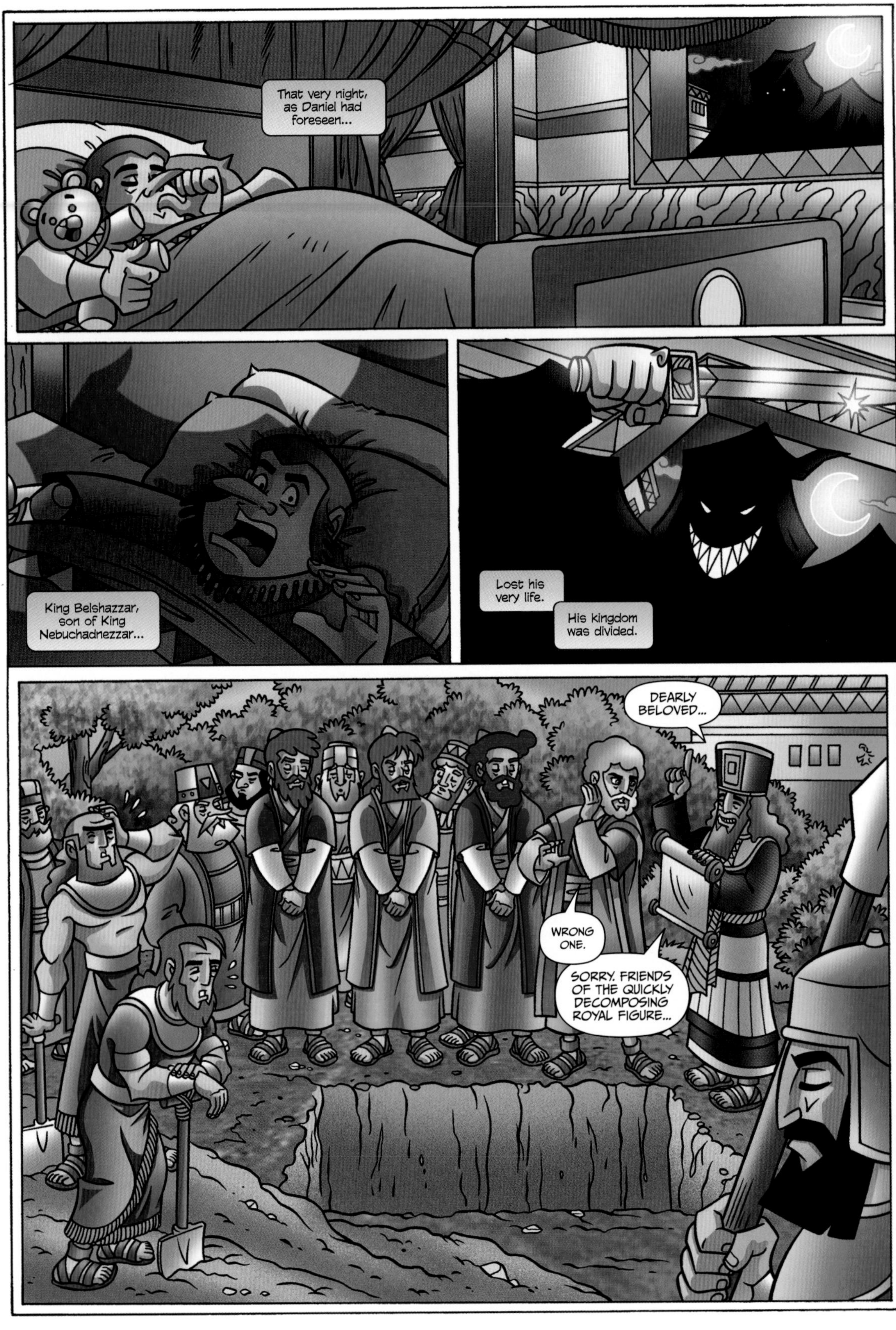
That very night, as Daniel had foreseen...
King Belshazzar, son of King Nebuchadnezzar...
Lost his very life.
His kingdom was divided.
DEARLY BELOVED...
WRONG ONE.
SORRY. FRIENDS OF THE QUICKLY DECOMPOSING ROYAL FIGURE...

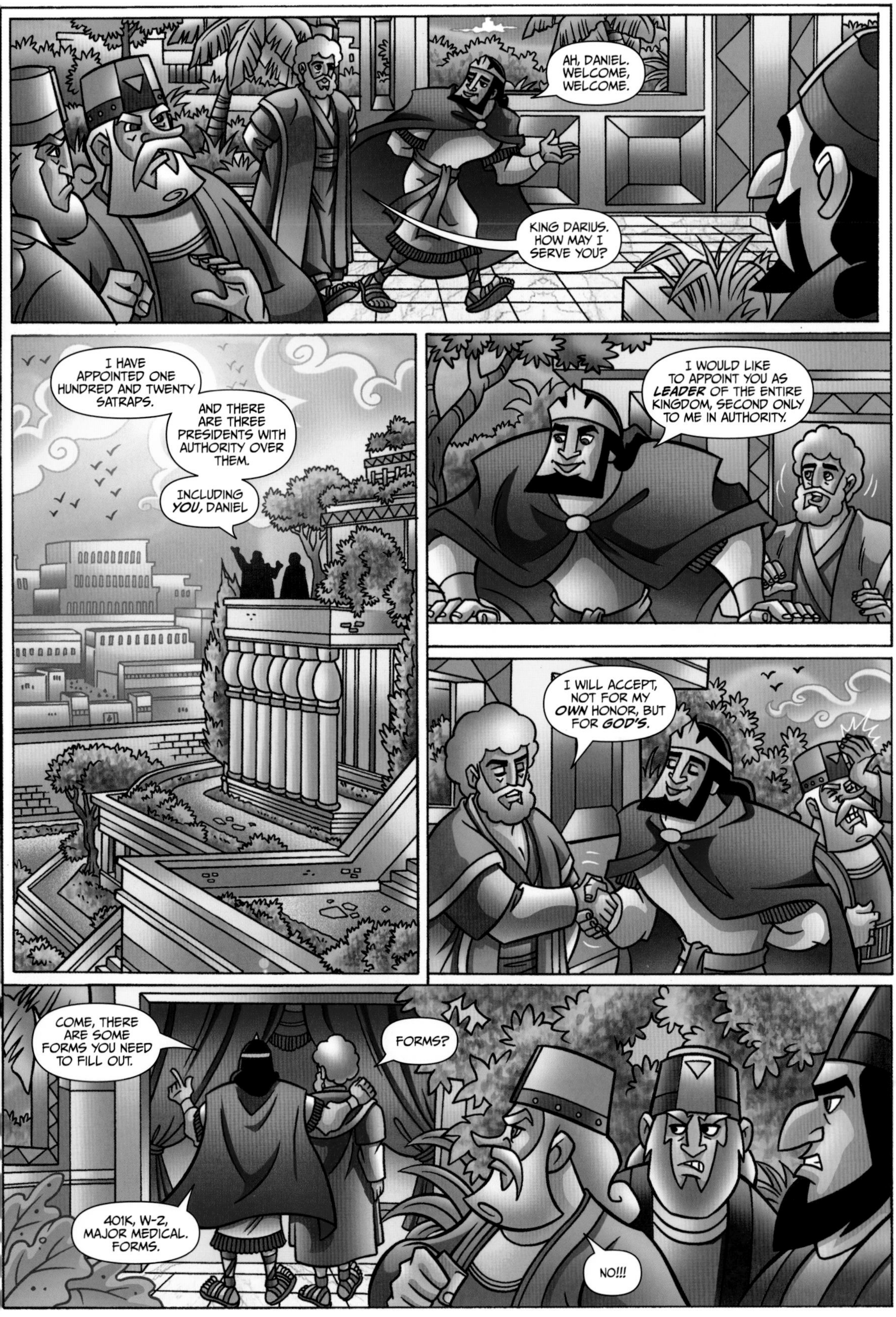
AH, DANIEL. WELCOME, WELCOME.
KING DARIUS. HOW MAY I SERVE YOU?
I HAVE APPOINTED ONE HUNDRED AND TWENTY SATRAPS.
AND THERE ARE THREE PRESIDENTS WITH AUTHORITY OVER THEM.
INCLUDING YOU, DANIEL
I WOULD LIKE TO APPOINT YOU AS LEADER OF THE ENTIRE KINGDOM, SECOND ONLY TO ME IN AUTHORITY.
I WILL ACCEPT, NOT FOR MY OWN HONOR, BUT FOR GOD'S.
COME, THERE ARE SOME FORMS YOU NEED TO FILL OUT.
FORMS?
401K, W-2, MAJOR MEDICAL. FORMS.
NO!!!

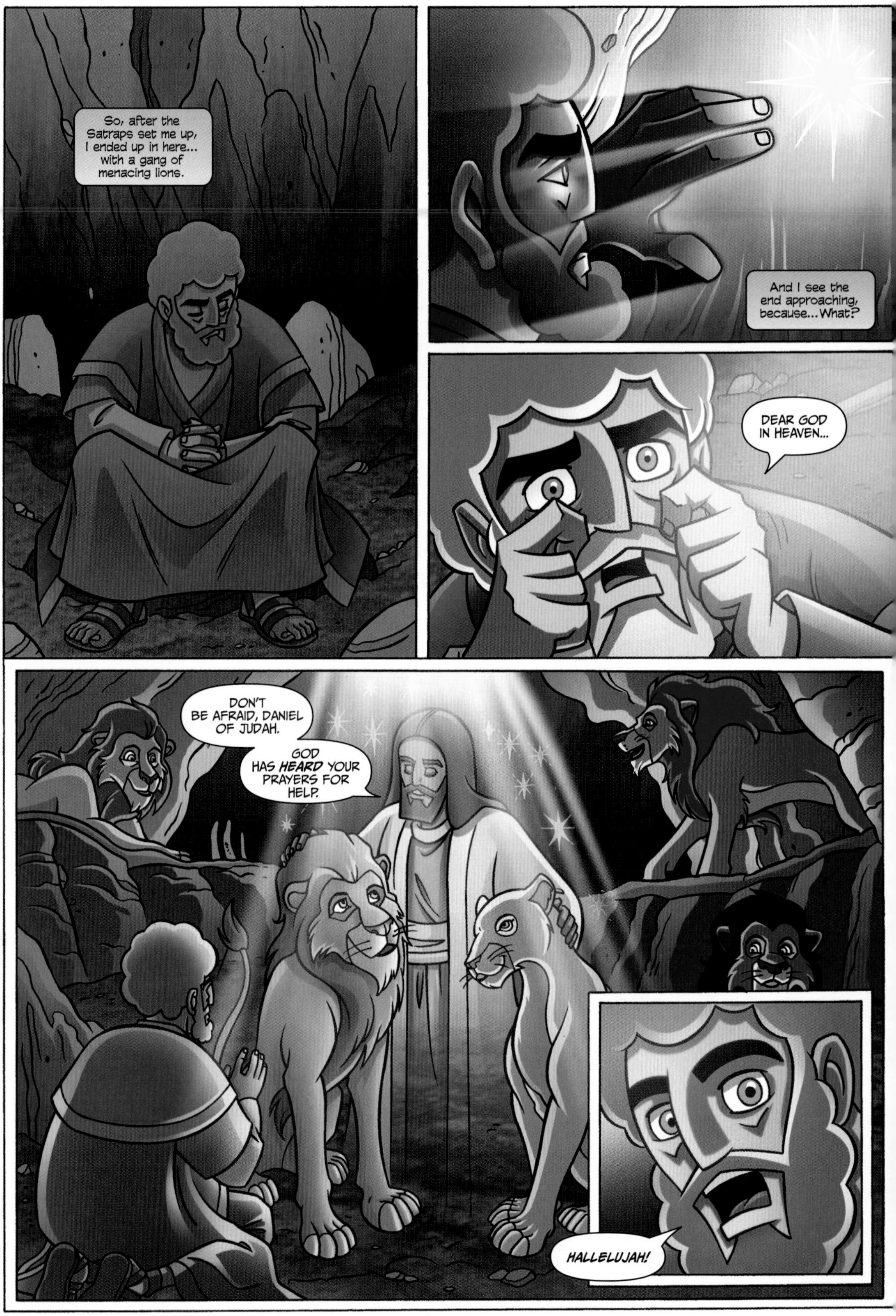
So, after the Satraps set me up, I ended up in here... with a gang of menacing lions.
And I see the end approaching, because... What?
DEAR GOD IN HEAVEN...
DON'T BE AFRAID, DANIEL OF JUDAH.
GOD HAS HEARD YOUR PRAYERS FOR HELP.
HALLELUJAH!

CHAPTER 7: THAT WHICH IS, WHICH WAS, AND THAT WHICH HAS YET TO COME

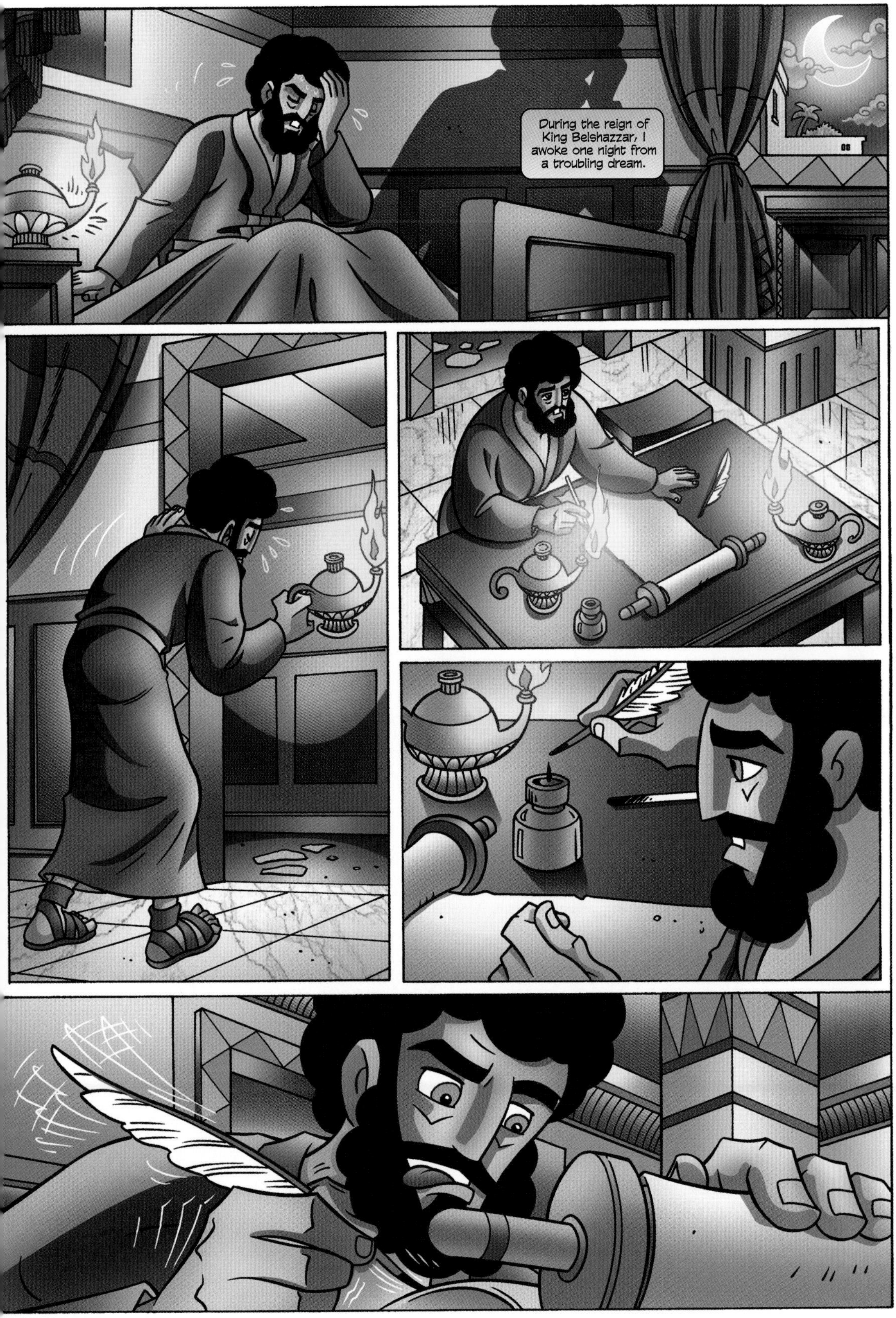
During the reign of King Belshazzar, I awoke one night from a troubling dream.

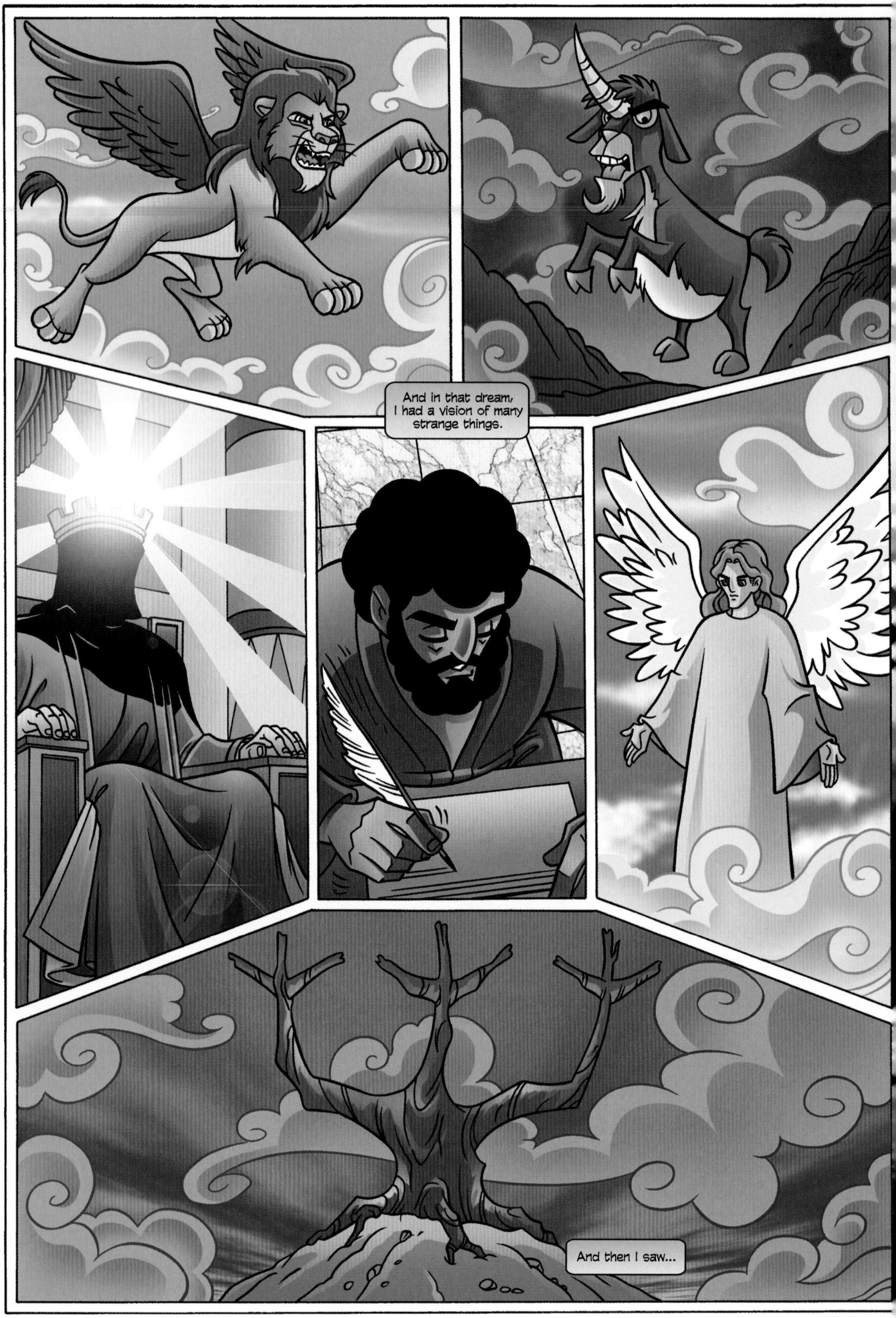
And in that dream, I had a vision of many strange things.
And then I saw...

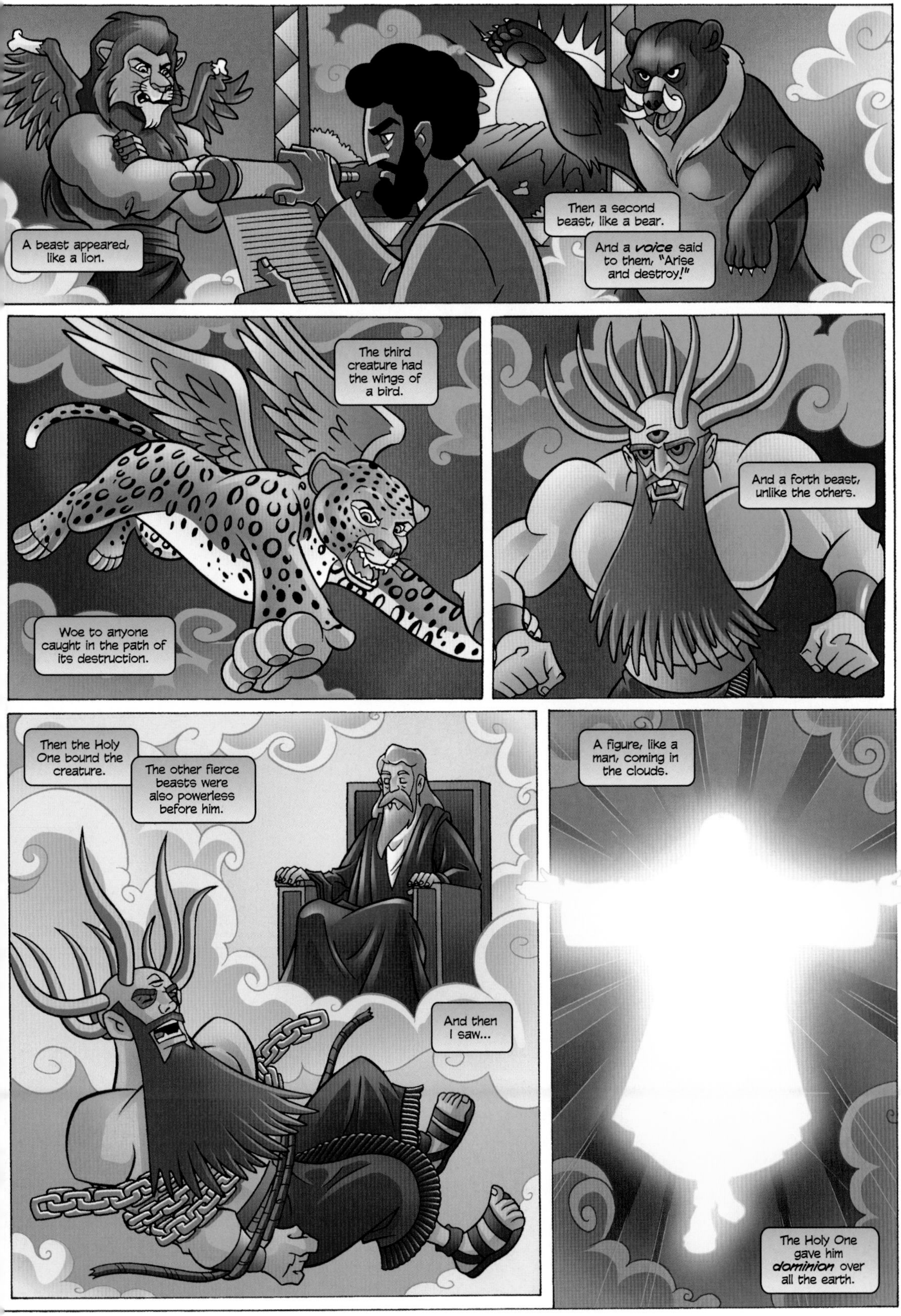

A beast appeared, like a lion.
Then a second beast, like a bear.
And a voice said to them, "Arise and destroy!"
The third creature had the wings of a bird.
Woe to anyone caught in the path of its destruction.
And a forth beast, unlike the others.
Then the Holy One bound the creature.
The other fierce beasts were also powerless before him.
And then I saw...
A figure, like a man, coming in the clouds.
The Holy One gave him dominion over all the earth.

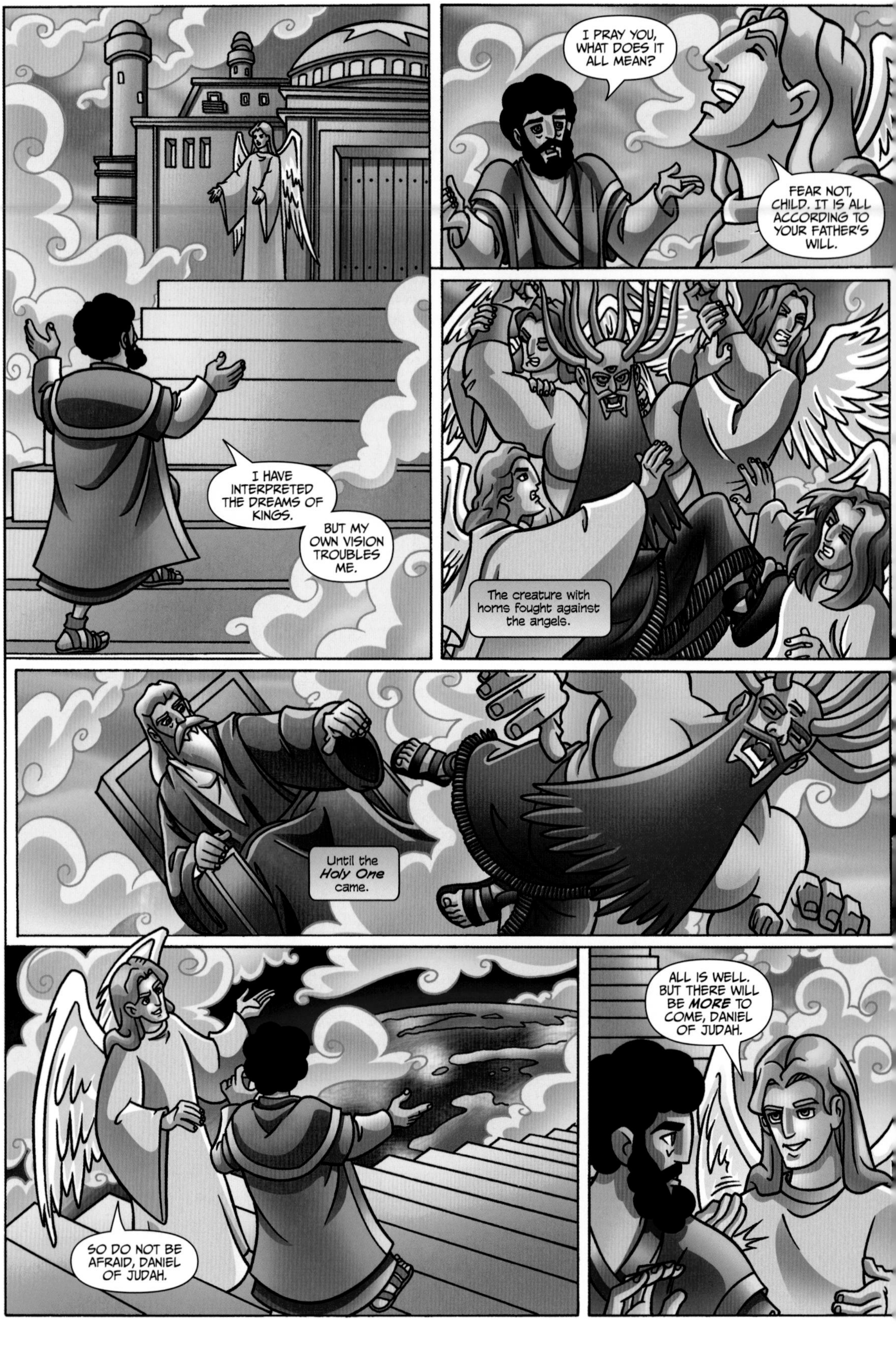
I HAVE INTERPRETED THE DREAMS OF KINGS.
BUT MY OWN VISION TROUBLES ME.
I PRAY YOU, WHAT DOES IT ALL MEAN?
FEAR NOT, CHILD. IT IS ALL ACCORDING TO YOUR FATHER'S WILL.
The creature with horns fought against the angels.
Until the *Holy One* came.
SO DO NOT BE AFRAID, DANIEL OF JUDAH.
ALL IS WELL. BUT THERE WILL BE *MORE* TO COME, DANIEL OF JUDAH.

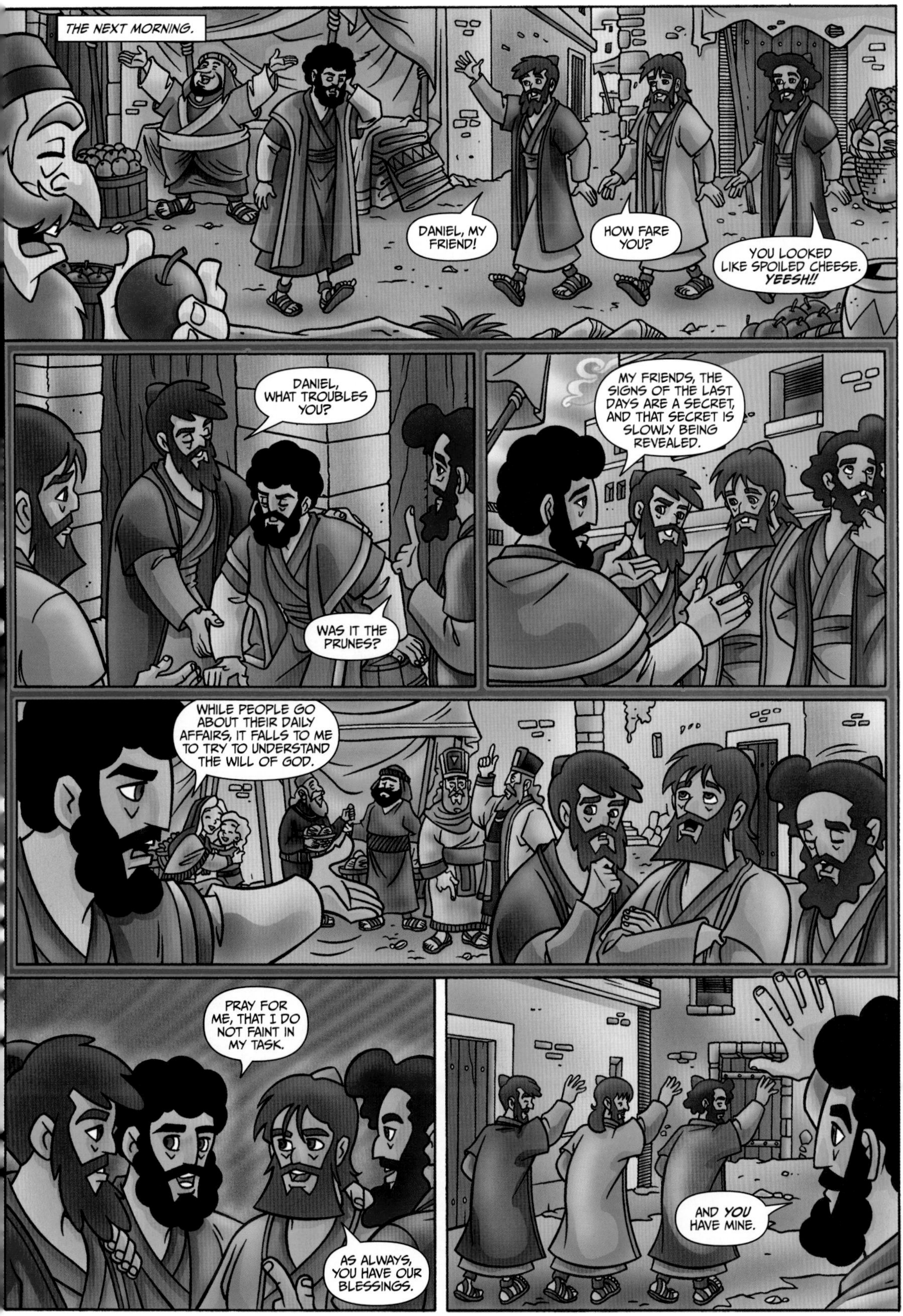
THE NEXT MORNING.
DANIEL, MY FRIEND!
HOW FARE YOU?
YOU LOOKED LIKE SPOILED CHEESE. YEESH!!
DANIEL, WHAT TROUBLES YOU?
WAS IT THE PRUNES?
MY FRIENDS, THE SIGNS OF THE LAST DAYS ARE A SECRET, AND THAT SECRET IS SLOWLY BEING REVEALED.
WHILE PEOPLE GO ABOUT THEIR DAILY AFFAIRS, IT FALLS TO ME TO TRY TO UNDERSTAND THE WILL OF GOD.
PRAY FOR ME, THAT I DO NOT FAINT IN MY TASK.
AS ALWAYS, YOU HAVE OUR BLESSINGS.
AND YOU HAVE MINE.

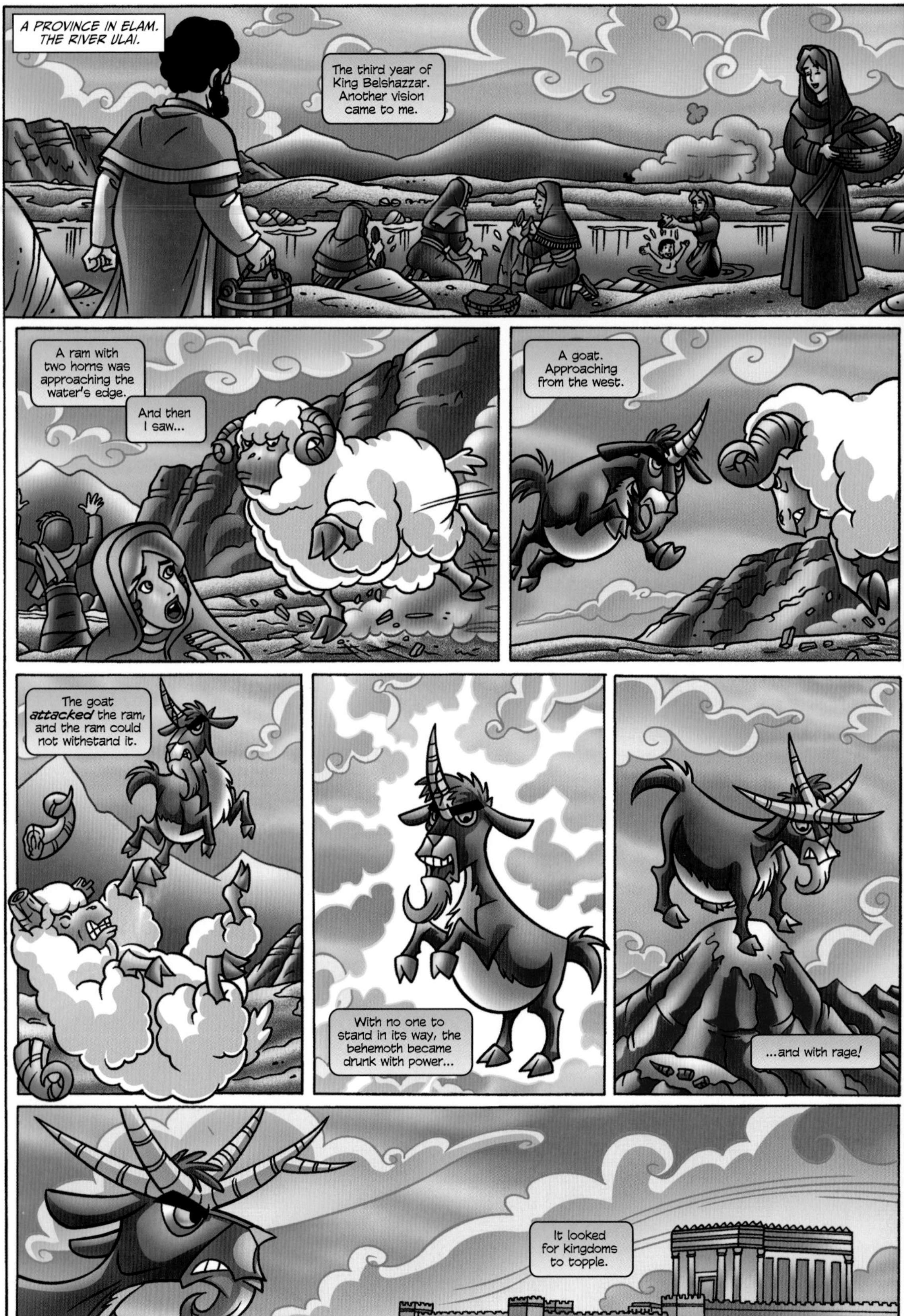
A PROVINCE IN ELAM. THE RIVER ULAI.
The third year of King Belshazzar. Another vision came to me.
A ram with two horns was approaching the water's edge.
And then I saw...
A goat. Approaching from the west.
The goat *attacked* the ram, and the ram could not withstand it.
With no one to stand in its way, the behemoth became drunk with power...
...and with rage!
It looked for kingdoms to topple.

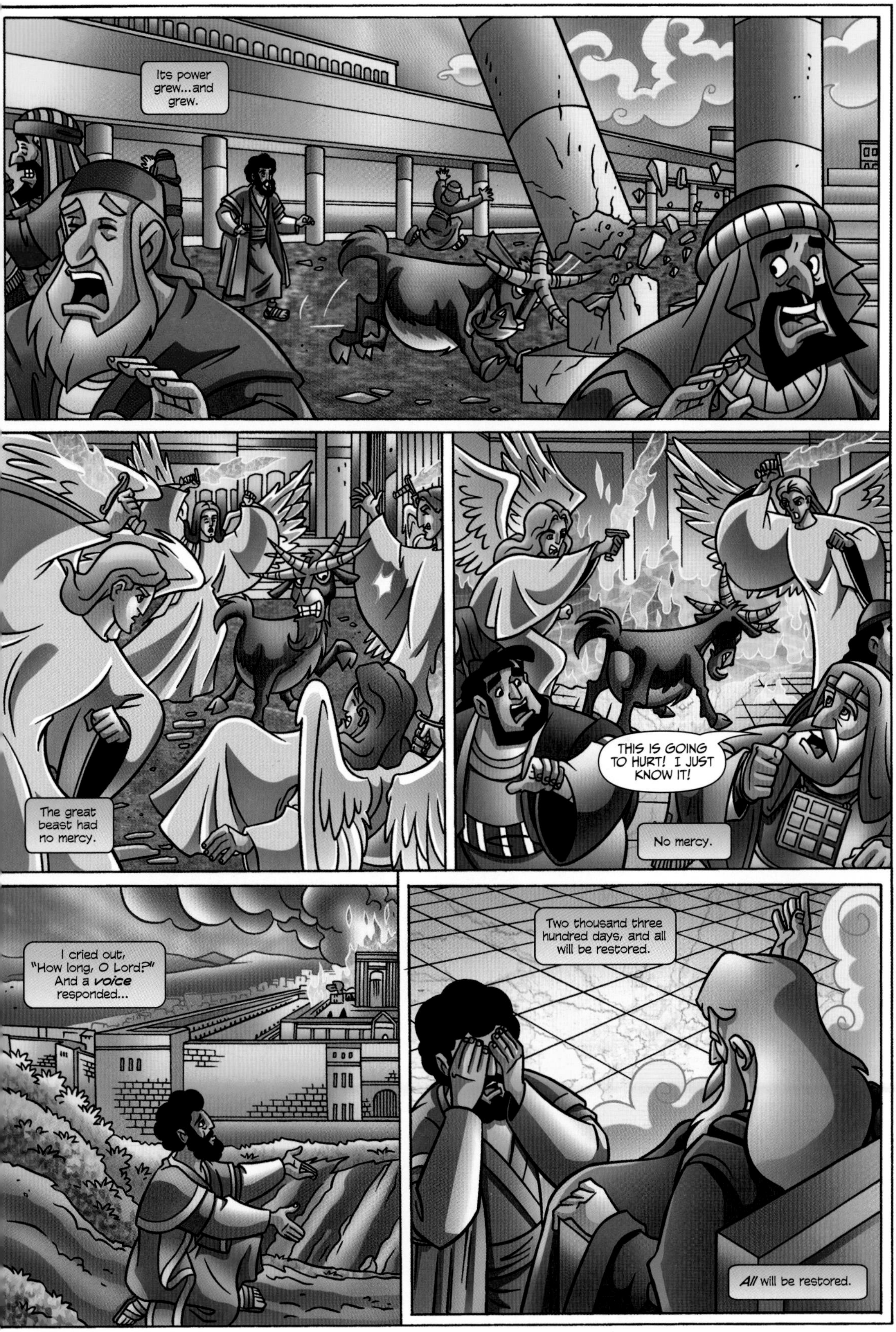
Its power grew...and grew.
The great beast had no mercy.
THIS IS GOING TO HURT! I JUST KNOW IT!
No mercy.
I cried out, "How long, O Lord?" And a *voice* responded...
Two thousand three hundred days, and all will be restored.
All will be restored.

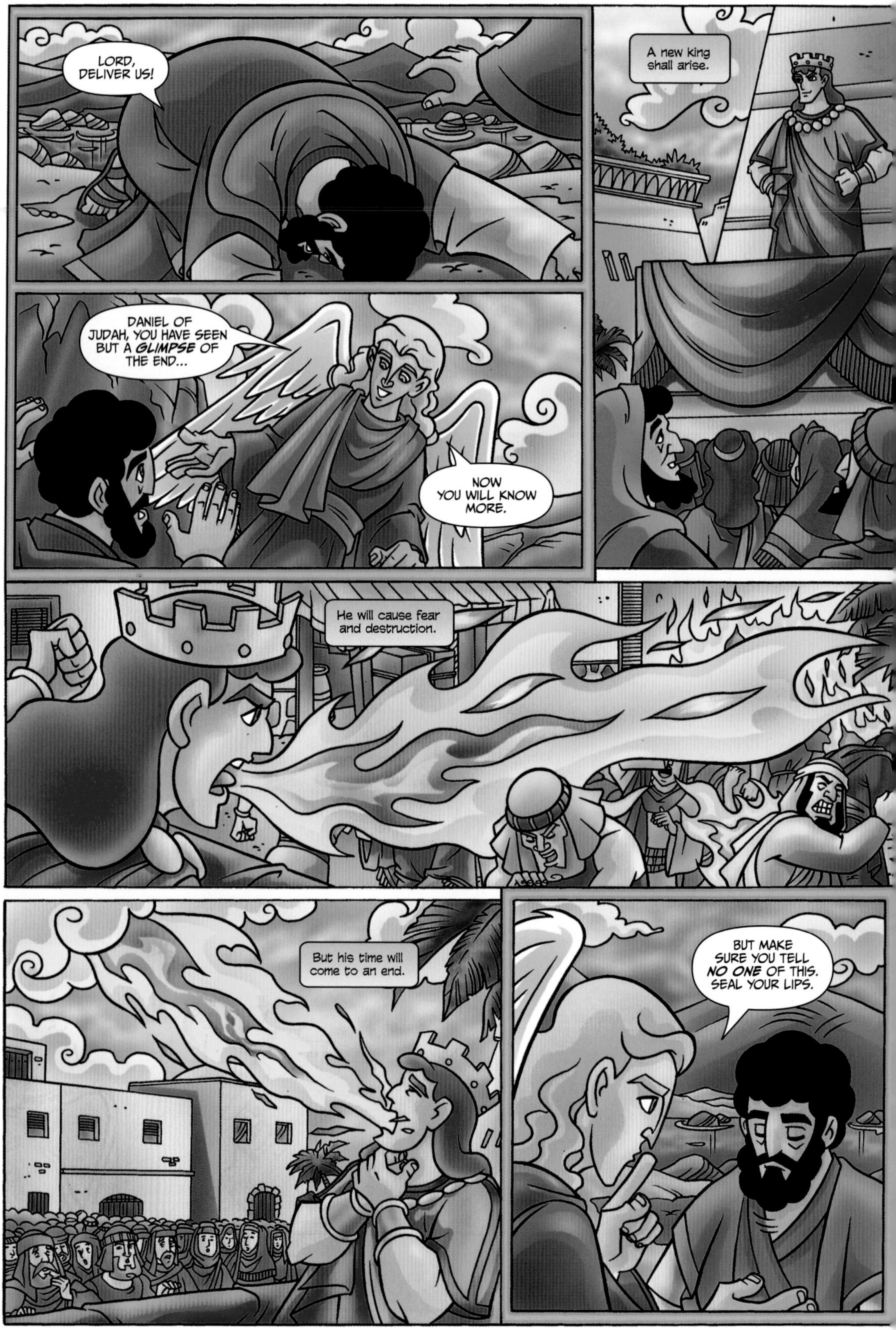

LORD, DELIVER US!
A new king shall arise.
DANIEL OF JUDAH, YOU HAVE SEEN BUT A *GLIMPSE* OF THE END...
NOW YOU WILL KNOW MORE.
He will cause fear and destruction.
But his time will come to an end.
BUT MAKE SURE YOU TELL ***NO ONE*** OF THIS. SEAL YOUR LIPS.

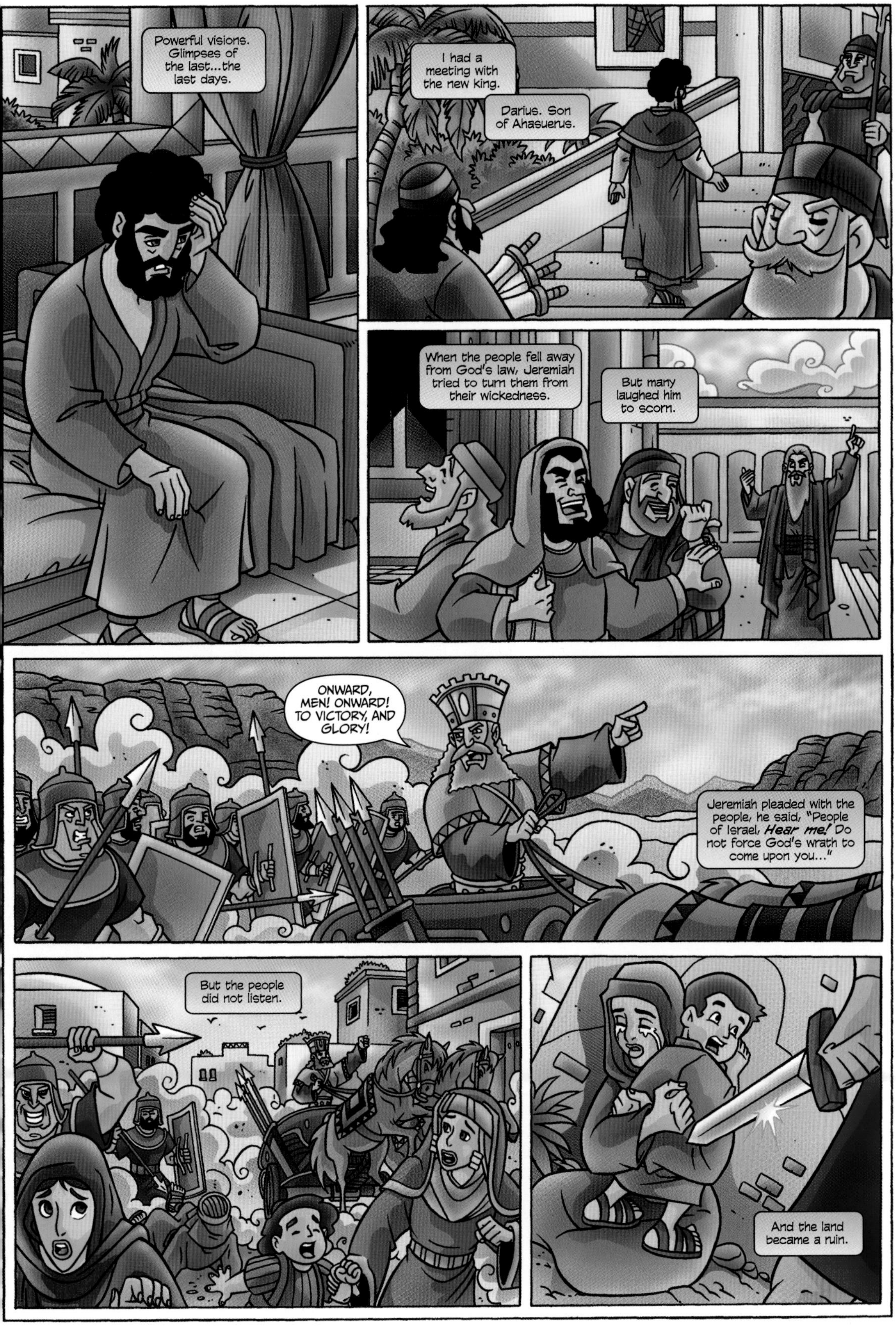
Powerful visions. Glimpses of the last...the last days.
I had a meeting with the new king.
Darius. Son of Ahasuerus.
When the people fell away from God's law, Jeremiah tried to turn them from their wickedness.
But many laughed him to scorn.
ONWARD, MEN! ONWARD! TO VICTORY, AND GLORY!
Jeremiah pleaded with the people, he said, "People of Israel, *Hear me!* Do not force God's wrath to come upon you..."
But the people did not listen.
And the land became a ruin.

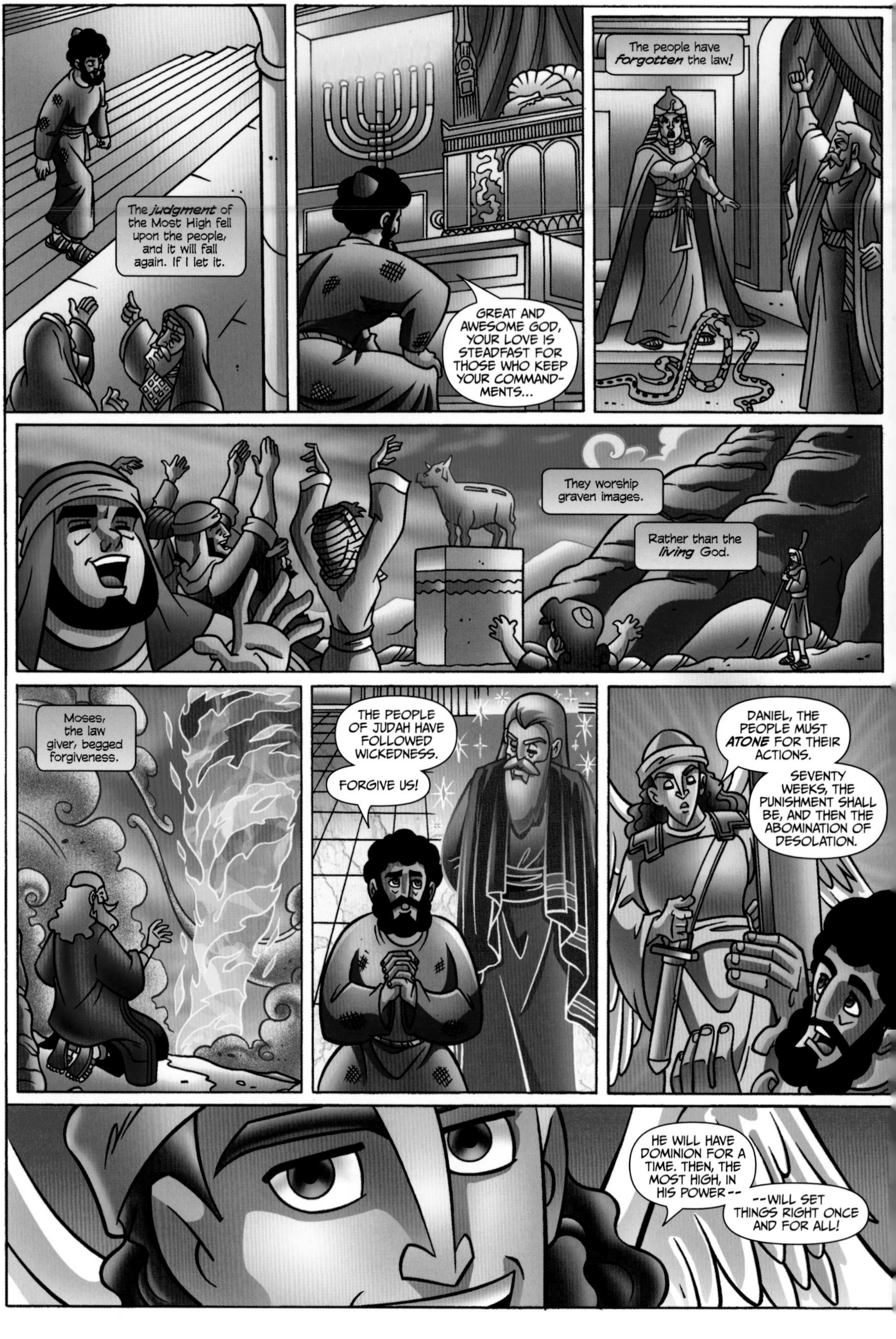
The *judgment* of the Most High fell upon the people, and it will fall again. If I let it.
GREAT AND AWESOME GOD, YOUR LOVE IS STEADFAST FOR THOSE WHO KEEP YOUR COMMAND-MENTS...
The people have *forgotten* the law!
They worship graven images.
Rather than the *living* God.
Moses, the law giver, begged forgiveness.
THE PEOPLE OF JUDAH HAVE FOLLOWED WICKEDNESS.
FORGIVE US!
DANIEL, THE PEOPLE MUST *ATONE* FOR THEIR ACTIONS.
SEVENTY WEEKS, THE PUNISHMENT SHALL BE, AND THEN THE ABOMINATION OF DESOLATION.
HE WILL HAVE DOMINION FOR A TIME. THEN, THE MOST HIGH, IN HIS POWER--
--WILL SET THINGS RIGHT ONCE AND FOR ALL!

CHAPTER 8: THE SECRETS OF ANGELS

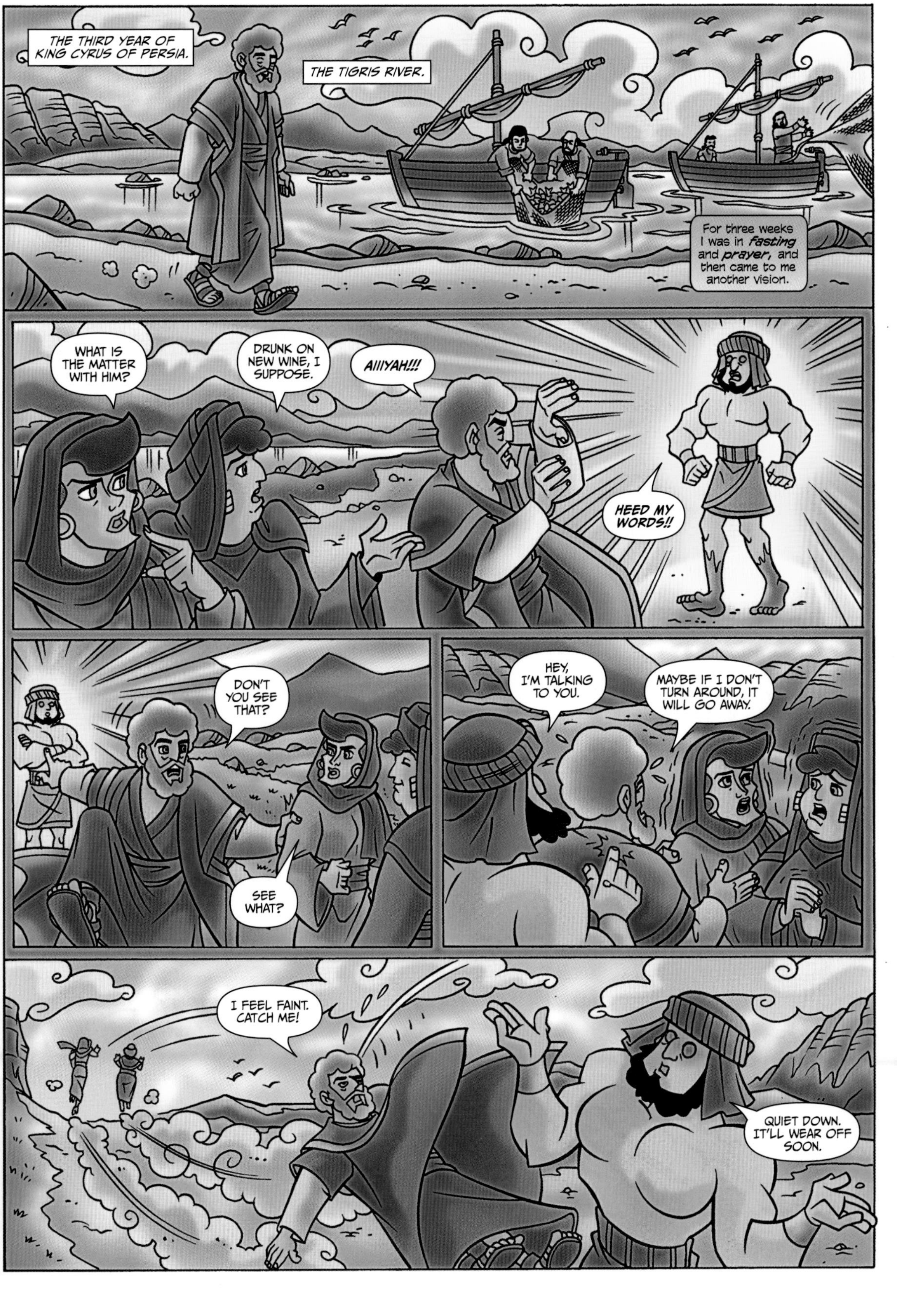
THE THIRD YEAR OF KING CYRUS OF PERSIA.
THE TIGRIS RIVER.
For three weeks I was in *fasting* and *prayer,* and then came to me another vision.
WHAT IS THE MATTER WITH HIM?
DRUNK ON NEW WINE, I SUPPOSE.
AIIIYAH!!!
HEED MY WORDS!!
DON'T YOU SEE THAT?
SEE WHAT?
HEY, I'M TALKING TO YOU.
MAYBE IF I DON'T TURN AROUND, IT WILL GO AWAY.
I FEEL FAINT. CATCH ME!
QUIET DOWN. IT'LL WEAR OFF SOON.

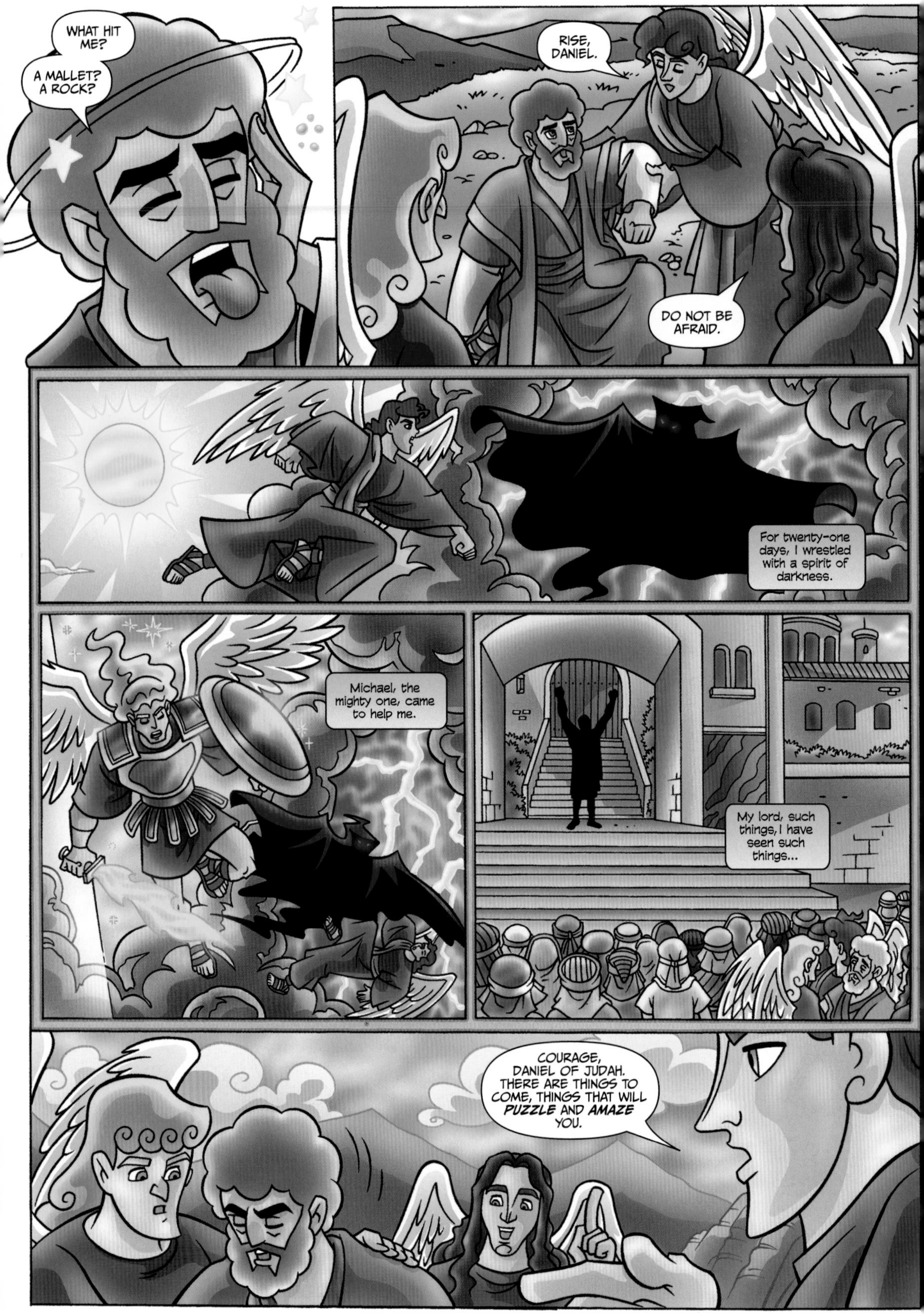
WHAT HIT ME?
A MALLET? A ROCK?
RISE, DANIEL.
DO NOT BE AFRAID.
For twenty-one days, I wrestled with a spirit of darkness.
Michael, the mighty one, came to help me.
My lord, such things, I have seen such things...
COURAGE, DANIEL OF JUDAH. THERE ARE THINGS TO COME, THINGS THAT WILL *PUZZLE* AND *AMAZE* YOU.

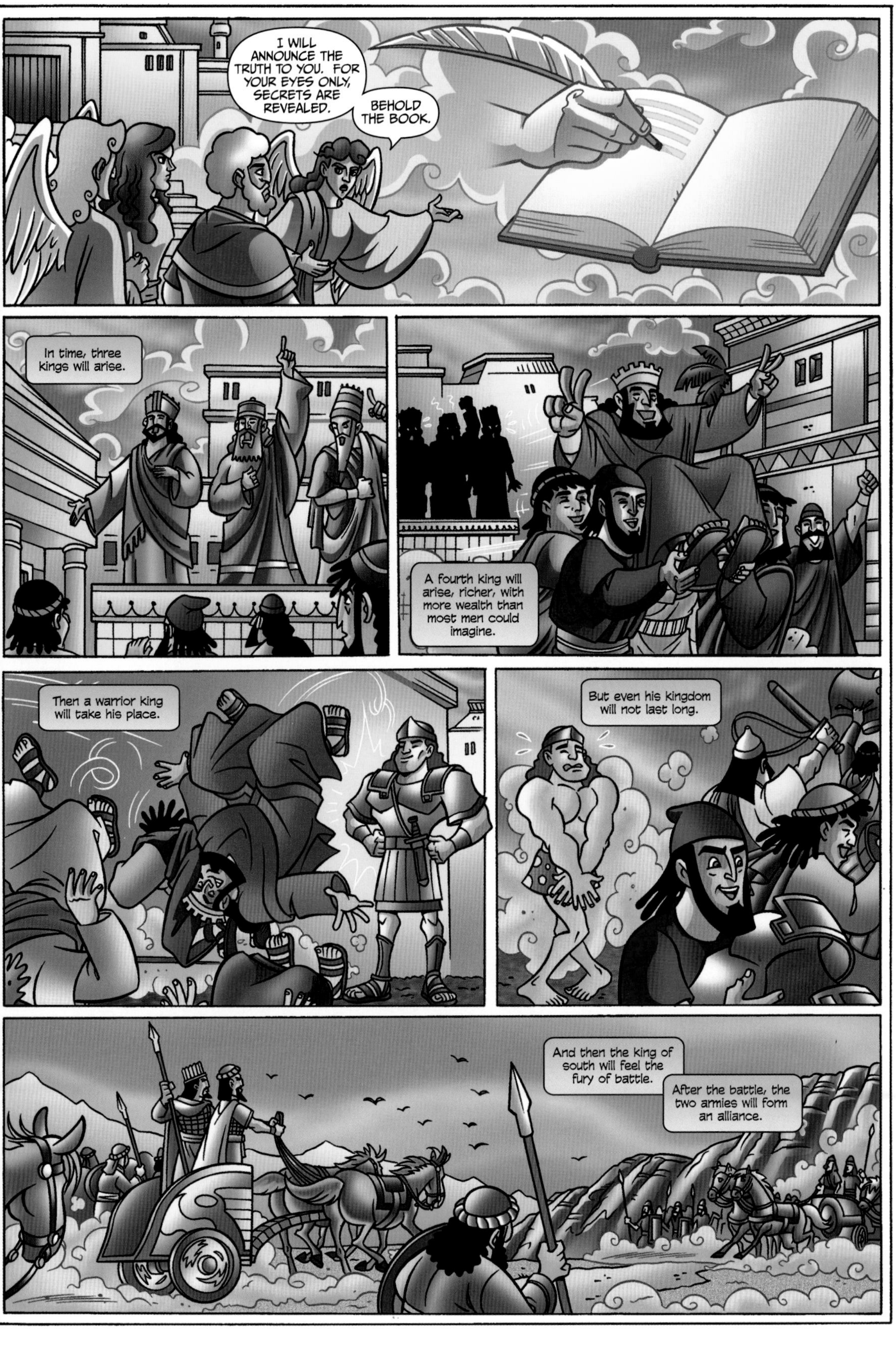
I WILL ANNOUNCE THE TRUTH TO YOU. FOR YOUR EYES ONLY, SECRETS ARE REVEALED.
BEHOLD THE BOOK.
In time, three kings will arise.
A fourth king will arise, richer, with more wealth than most men could imagine.
Then a warrior king will take his place.
But even his kingdom will not last long.
And then the king of south will feel the fury of battle.
After the battle, the two armies will form an alliance.

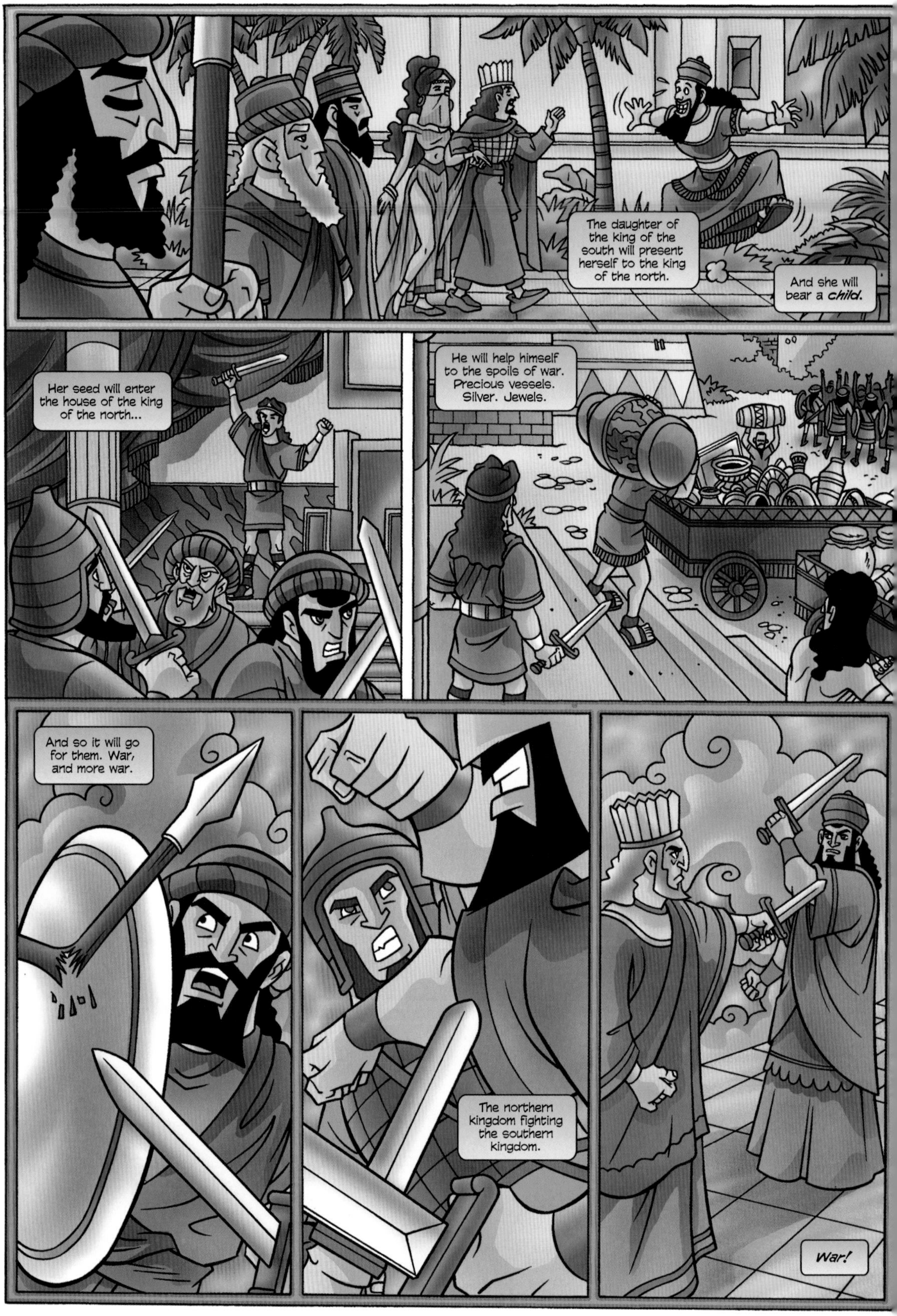
The daughter of the king of the south will present herself to the king of the north.
And she will bear a *child*.
Her seed will enter the house of the king of the north...
He will help himself to the spoils of war. Precious vessels. Silver. Jewels.
And so it will go for them. War, and more war.
The northern kingdom fighting the southern kingdom.
War!

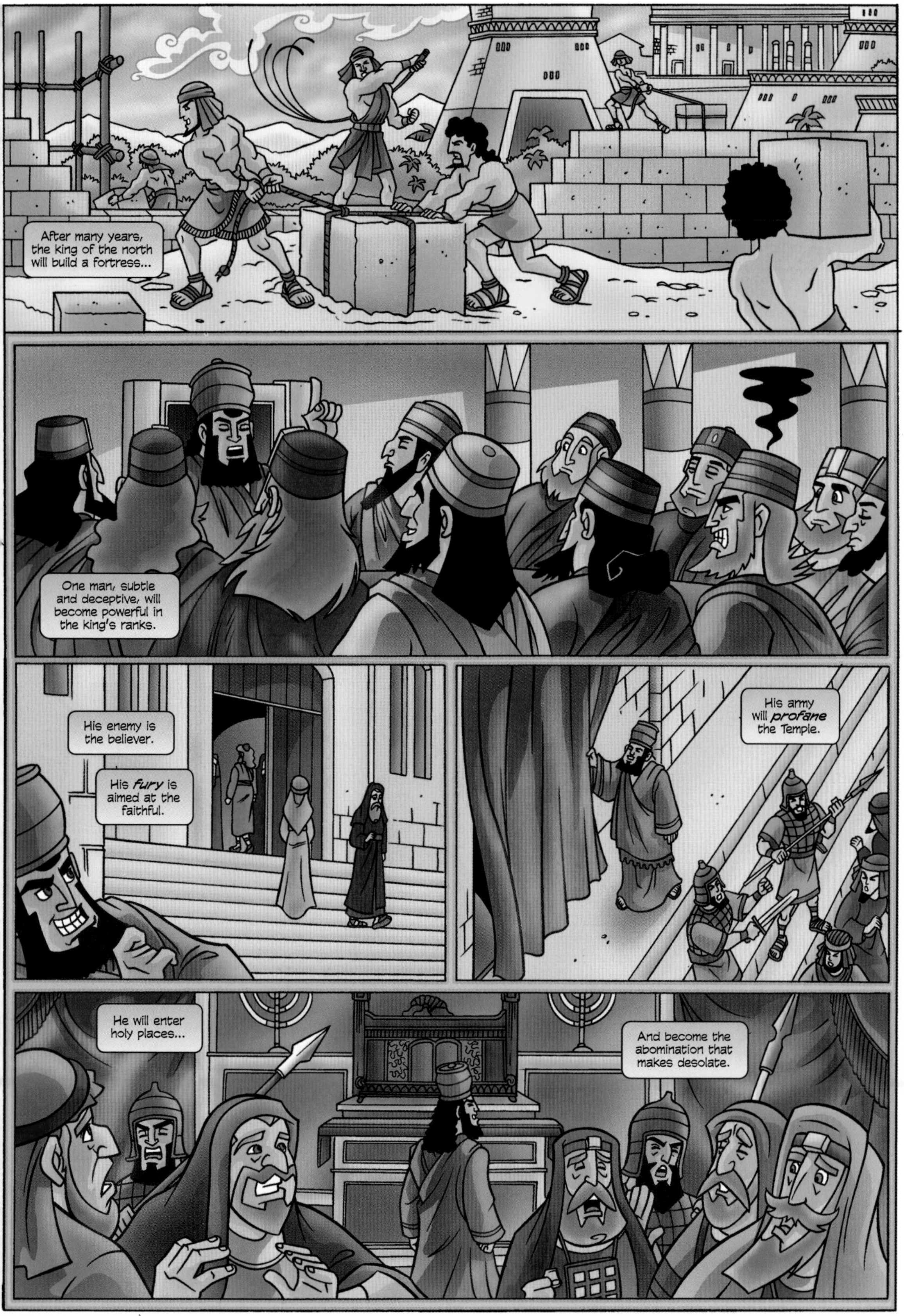
After many years, the king of the north will build a fortress...
One man, subtle and deceptive, will become powerful in the king's ranks.
His enemy is the believer.
His *fury* is aimed at the faithful.
His army will *profane* the Temple.
He will enter holy places...
And become the abomination that makes desolate.

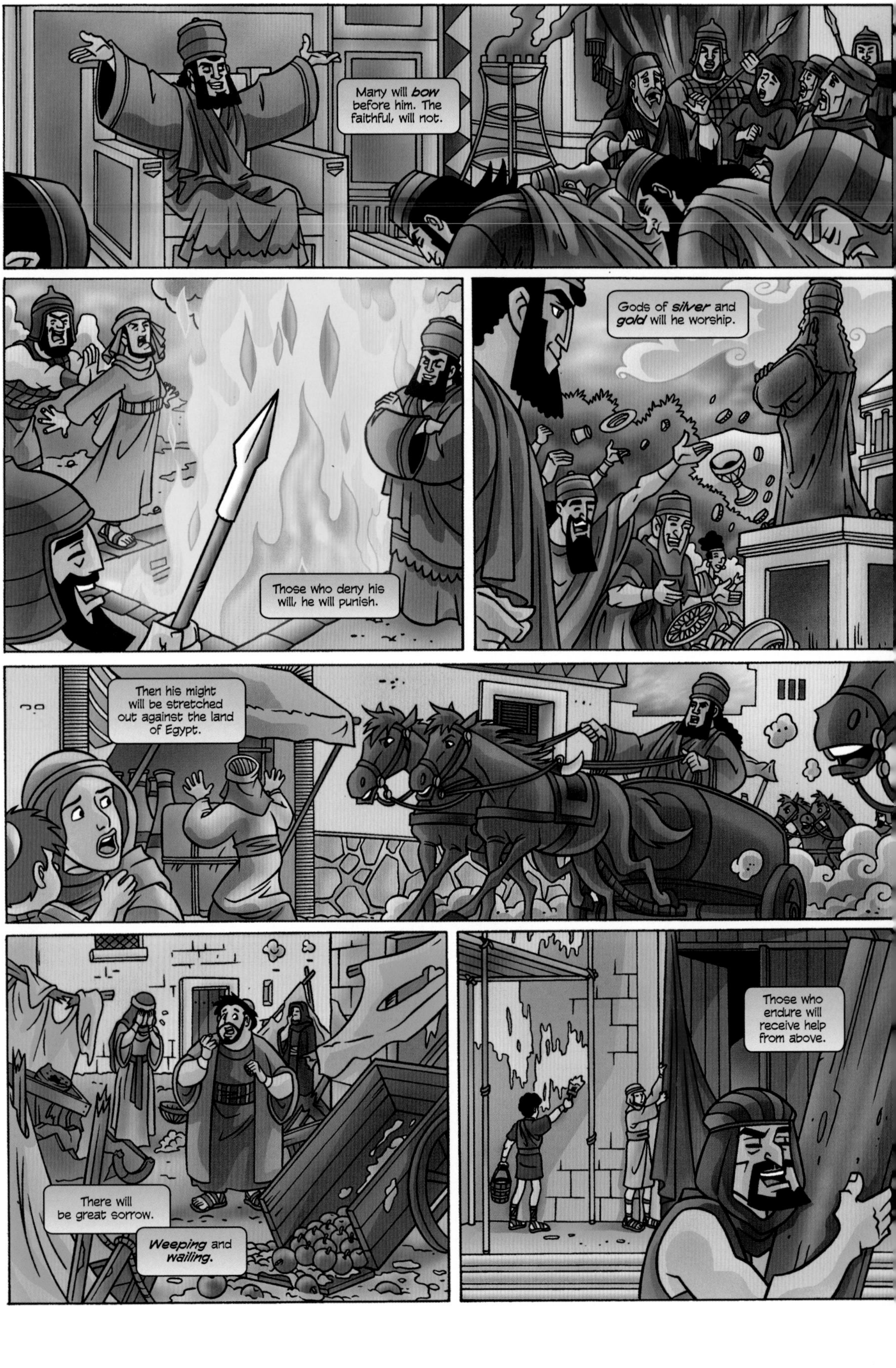
Many will *bow* before him. The faithful, will not.
Those who deny his will, he will punish.
Gods of *silver* and *gold* will he worship.
Then his might will be stretched out against the land of Egypt.
There will be great sorrow.
Weeping and *wailing*.
Those who endure will receive help from above.

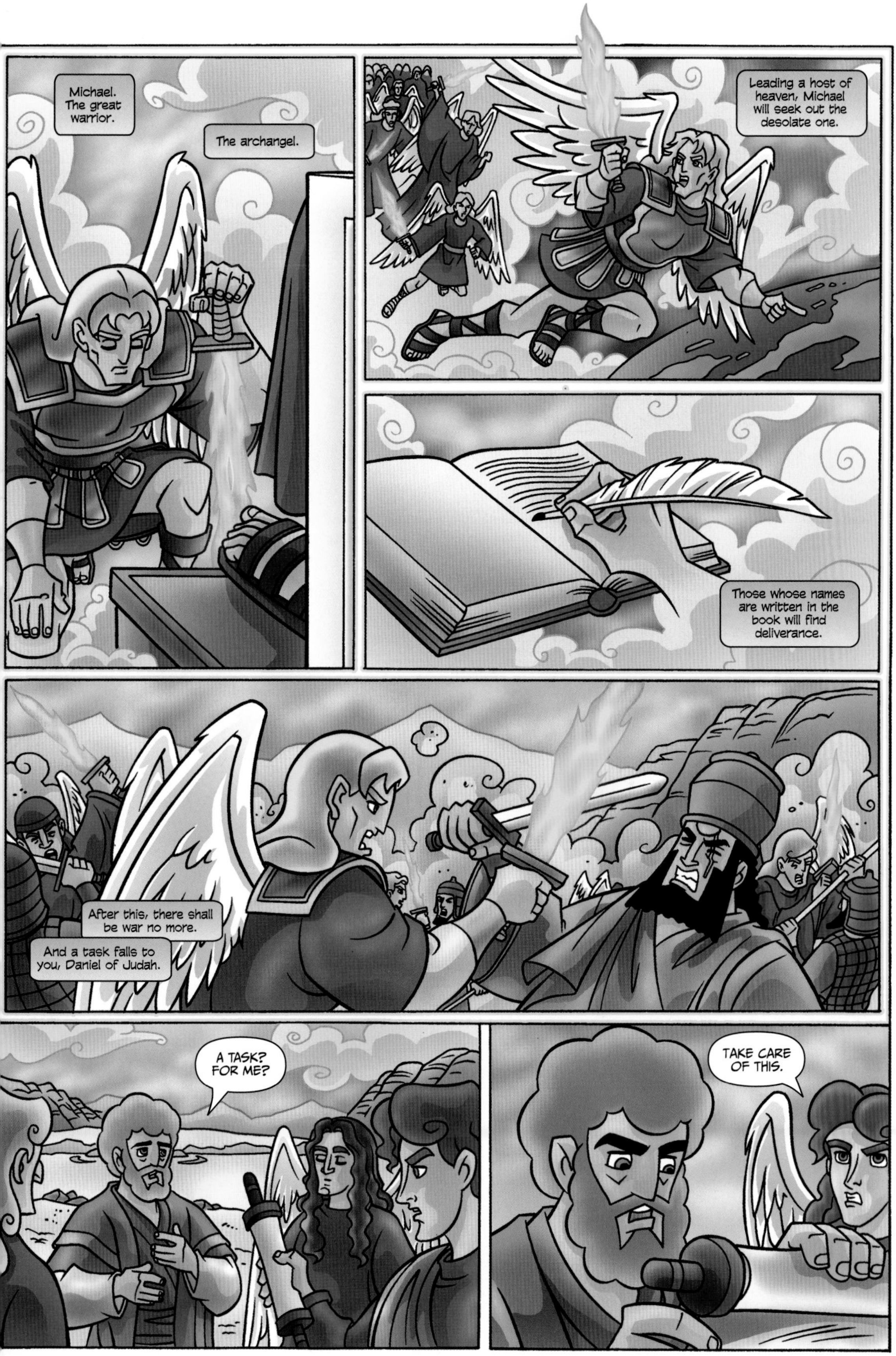

Michael. The great warrior.
The archangel.
Leading a host of heaven, Michael will seek out the desolate one.
Those whose names are written in the book will find deliverance.
After this, there shall be war no more.
And a task falls to you, Daniel of Judah.
A TASK? FOR ME?
TAKE CARE OF THIS.

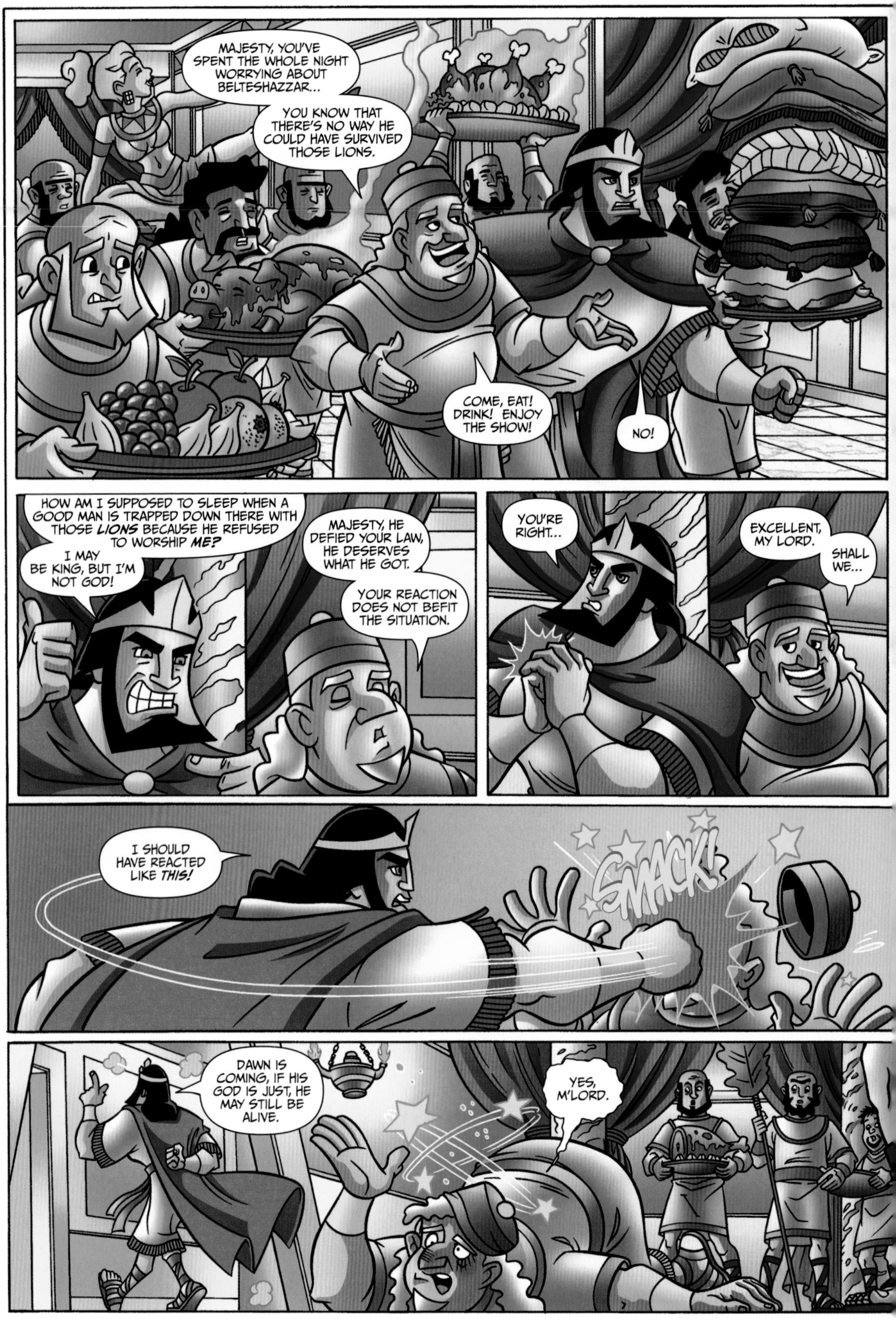
MAJESTY, YOU'VE SPENT THE WHOLE NIGHT WORRYING ABOUT BELTESHAZZAR...
YOU KNOW THAT THERE'S NO WAY HE COULD HAVE SURVIVED THOSE LIONS.
COME, EAT! DRINK! ENJOY THE SHOW!
NO!
HOW AM I SUPPOSED TO SLEEP WHEN A GOOD MAN IS TRAPPED DOWN THERE WITH THOSE LIONS BECAUSE HE REFUSED TO WORSHIP ME?
I MAY BE KING, BUT I'M NOT GOD!
MAJESTY, HE DEFIED YOUR LAW, HE DESERVES WHAT HE GOT.
YOUR REACTION DOES NOT BEFIT THE SITUATION.
YOU'RE RIGHT...
EXCELLENT, MY LORD.
SHALL WE...
I SHOULD HAVE REACTED LIKE THIS!
SMACK!
DAWN IS COMING, IF HIS GOD IS JUST, HE MAY STILL BE ALIVE.
YES, M'LORD.

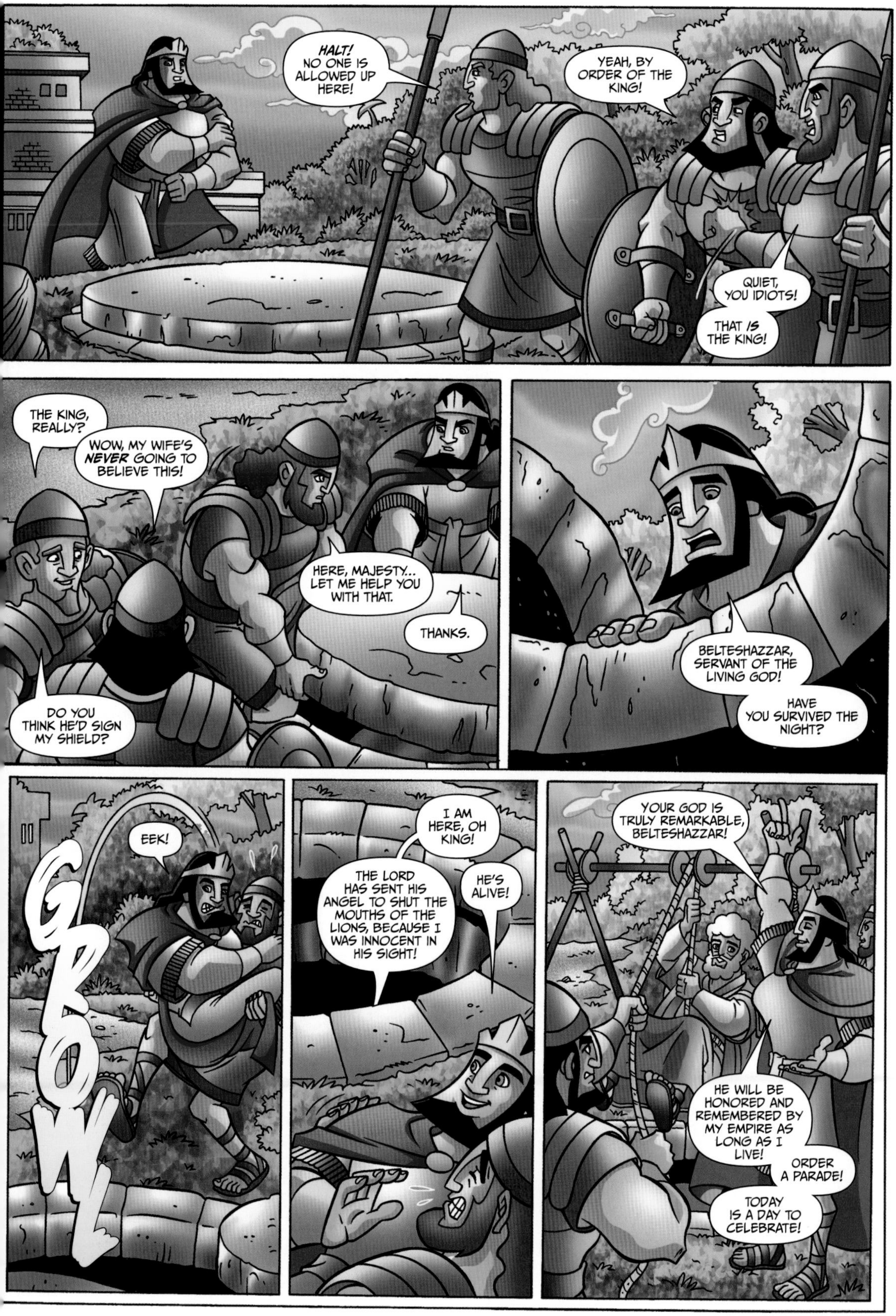

HALT! NO ONE IS ALLOWED UP HERE!
YEAH, BY ORDER OF THE KING!
QUIET, YOU IDIOTS!
THAT IS THE KING!
THE KING, REALLY?
WOW, MY WIFE'S NEVER GOING TO BELIEVE THIS!
HERE, MAJESTY... LET ME HELP YOU WITH THAT.
THANKS.
DO YOU THINK HE'D SIGN MY SHIELD?
BELTESHAZZAR, SERVANT OF THE LIVING GOD!
HAVE YOU SURVIVED THE NIGHT?
EEK!
GROWL
I AM HERE, OH KING!
THE LORD HAS SENT HIS ANGEL TO SHUT THE MOUTHS OF THE LIONS, BECAUSE I WAS INNOCENT IN HIS SIGHT!
HE'S ALIVE!
YOUR GOD IS TRULY REMARKABLE, BELTESHAZZAR!
HE WILL BE HONORED AND REMEMBERED BY MY EMPIRE AS LONG AS I LIVE!
ORDER A PARADE!
TODAY IS A DAY TO CELEBRATE!

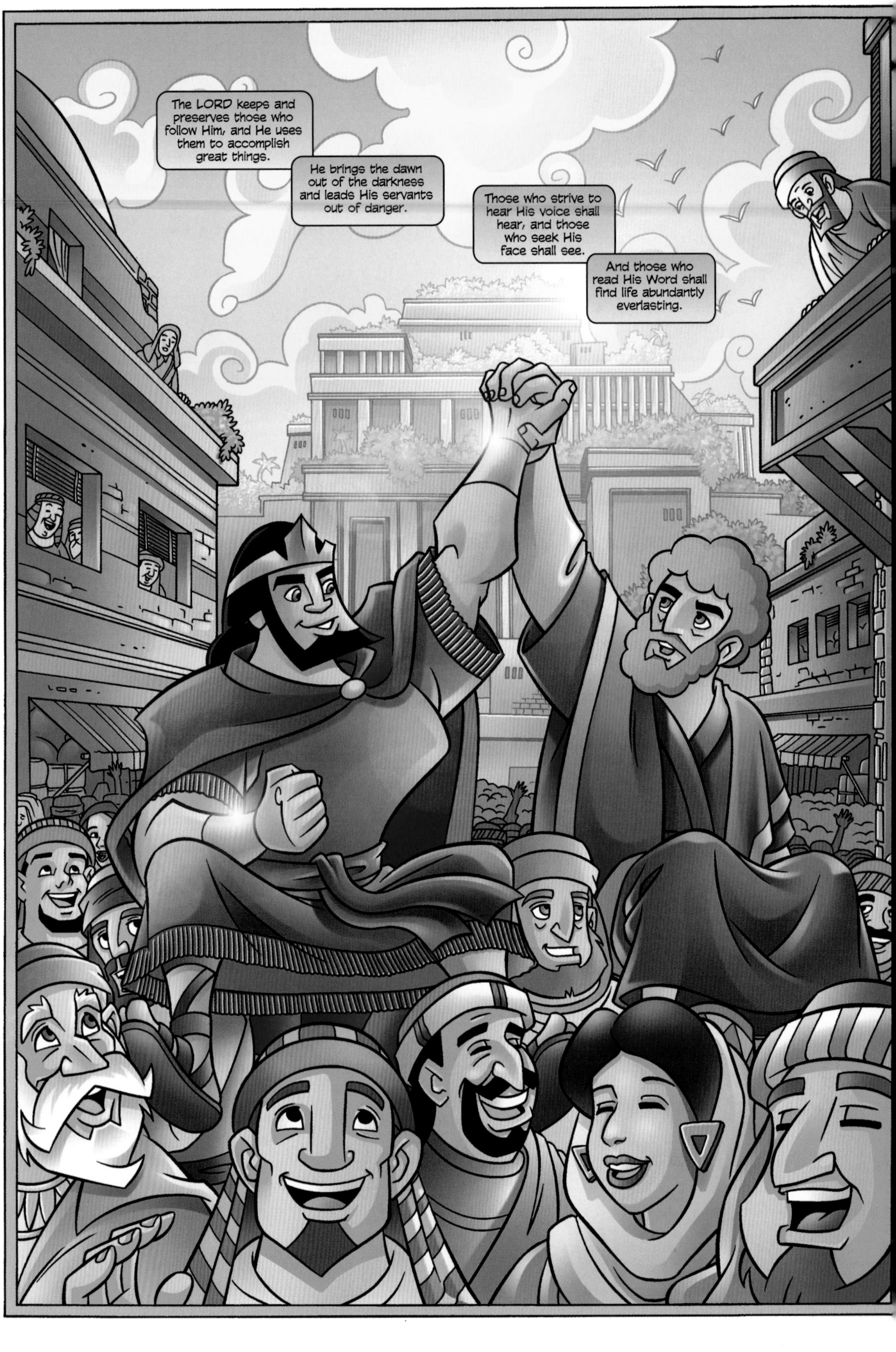

The LORD keeps and preserves those who follow Him, and He uses them to accomplish great things.
He brings the dawn out of the darkness and leads His servants out of danger.
Those who strive to hear His voice shall hear, and those who seek His face shall see.
And those who read His Word shall find life abundantly everlasting.

EPILOGUE:

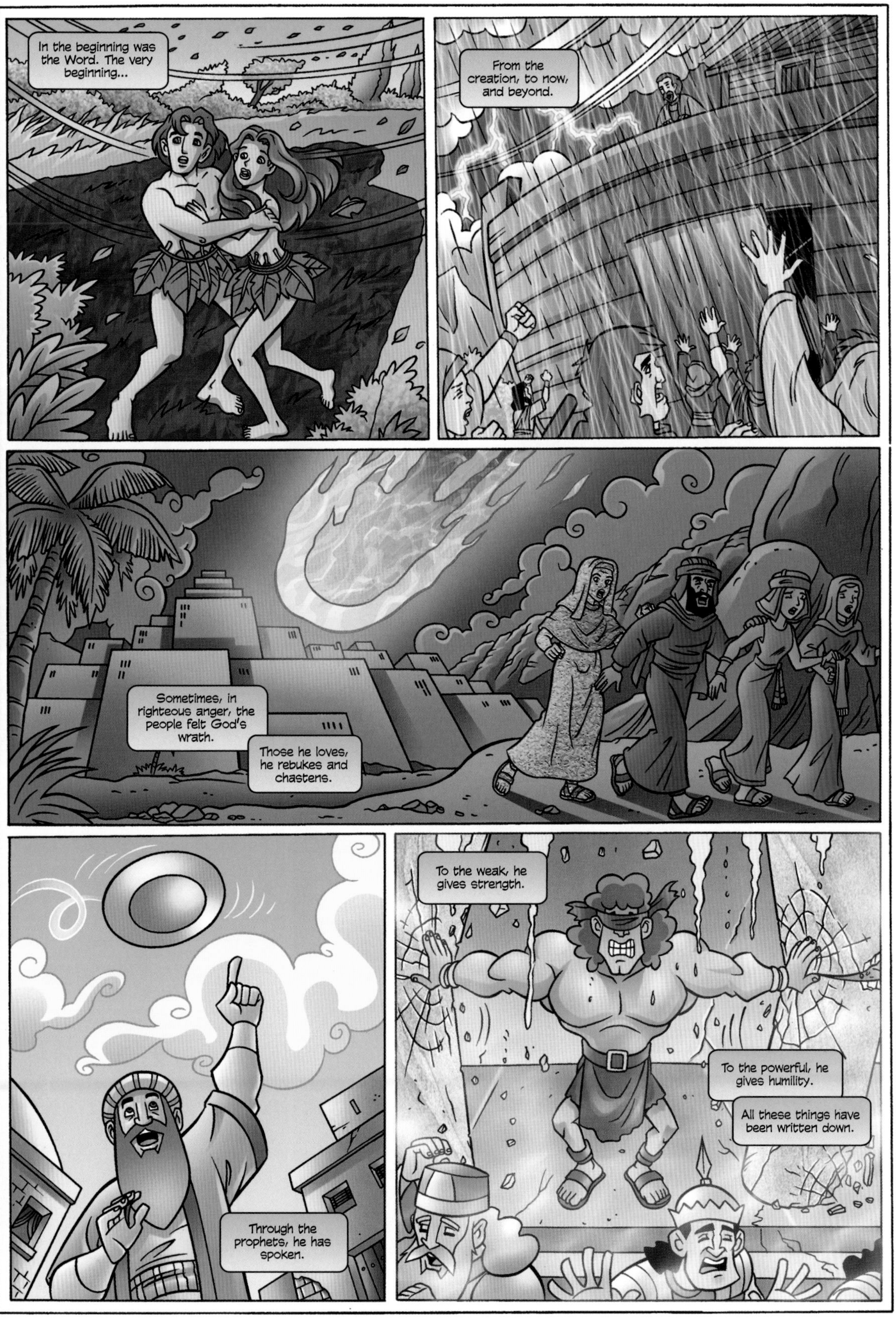
In the beginning was the Word. The very beginning...
From the creation, to now, and beyond.
Sometimes, in righteous anger, the people felt God's wrath.
Those he loves, he rebukes and chastens.
Through the prophets, he has spoken.
To the weak, he gives strength.
To the powerful, he gives humility.
All these things have been written down.

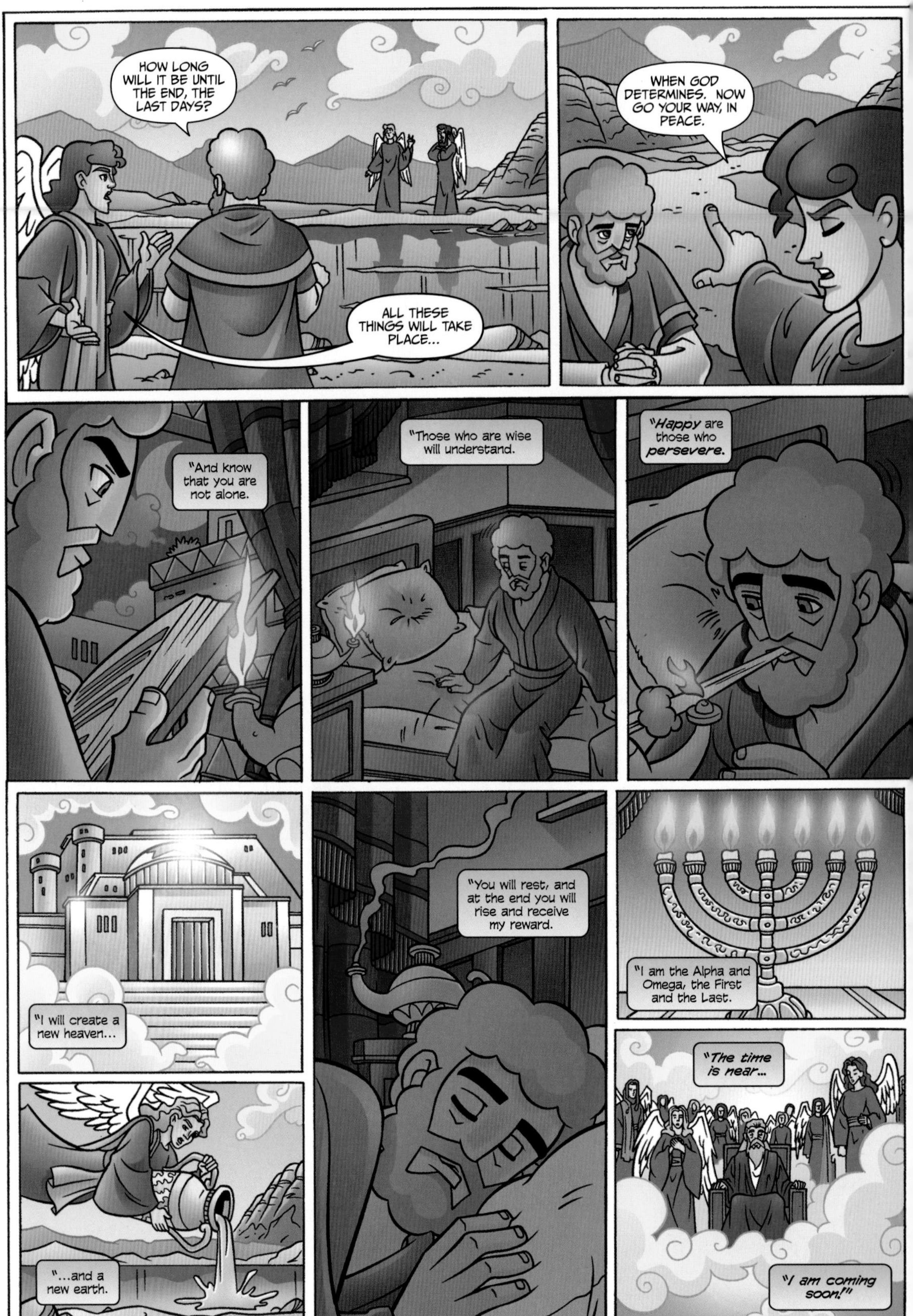
HOW LONG WILL IT BE UNTIL THE END, THE LAST DAYS?
ALL THESE THINGS WILL TAKE PLACE...
WHEN GOD DETERMINES. NOW GO YOUR WAY, IN PEACE.
"And know that you are not alone.
"Those who are wise will understand.
"Happy are those who persevere.
"I will create a new heaven...
"...and a new earth.
"You will rest, and at the end you will rise and receive my reward.
"I am the Alpha and Omega, the First and the Last.
"The time is near...
"I am coming soon!"

FIN